WAVERLY
inspirations
Your Guide to Personal Style

Meredith® Books
Des Moines, Iowa

Meredith® Press
An imprint of Meredith® Books

inspirations WAVERLY®
Your Guide to Personal Style

Editor: Vicki L. Ingham
Contributing Writer: Sharon Novotne O'Keefe
Art Director: Jerry J. Rank
Copy Chief: Catherine Hamrick
Copy and Production Editor: Terri Fredrickson
Contributing Copy Editor: Nancy A. Ruhling
Contributing Proofreaders: Kathy Eastman, Judith Friedman, Mary Pas
Electronic Production Coordinator: Paula Forest
Editorial and Design Assistants: Kaye Chabot, Mary Lee Gavin, Karen Schirm
Production Director: Douglas M. Johnston
Production Manager: Pam Kvitne
Assistant Prepress Manager: Marjorie J. Schenkelberg

Meredith® Books
Editor in Chief: James D. Blume
Design Director: Matt Strelecki
Managing Editor: Gregory H. Kayko
Executive Shelter Editor: Denise L. Caringer

Director, Sales & Marketing, Retail: Michael A. Peterson
Director, Sales & Marketing, Special Markets: Rita McMullen
Director, Sales & Marketing, Home & Garden Center Channel: Ray Wolf
Director, Operations: George A. Susral

Vice President, General Manager: Jamie L. Martin

Meredith Publishing Group
President, Publishing Group: Christopher M. Little
Vice President, Consumer Marketing & Development: Hal Oringer

Meredith Corporation
Chairman and Chief Executive Officer: William T. Kerr

Chairman of the Executive Committee: E. T. Meredith III

Waverly®
President: Christiane Michaels
Vice President, Creative Director: Albert Sardelli
Vice President of Marketing: Daniel J. Bonini
Director of Public Relations: Vicki Enteen

Cover Photograph: Oberti Gili.
The room shown is on page 144.

The editors of *Waverly® Inspirations* are dedicated to providing you with information and ideas to enhance your home. We welcome your comments and suggestions. Write to us at: Meredith Books, Shelter Department, 1716 Locust St., Des Moines, IA 50309-3023. Or visit our website at www.bhg.com.

Visit Waverly's website at www.decoratewaverly.com.
To find the location of the Waverly retailer or Waverly Home® Store nearest you, call 800/423-5881.

Waverly® is a registered trademark of F. Schumacher & Co.

Manufactured and distributed by Meredith Corporation
If you would like to purchase copies of any of our books, check wherever quality books are sold.

When it comes to decorating, the most important source of inspiration is *you*! The way you live, the things you love, and the kinds of colors, textures, and moods that naturally appeal to you are the most important ingredients in any decorating scheme. In fact, you inspire us at Waverly, not only to create harmonizing collections of fabric, wallpaper, paint, bed linens, and accessories, but also to provide trusted decorating advice—to help you have things your way at home. We call it *Waverly—Your Interior Design*.

This book is not a catalog but a decorating guide that starts by helping you learn more about yourself. Is your decorating personality Past Perfect, Town and Country, Modern Living, Beautiful Things—or a blend of one or more of these? Our fun quiz in Chapter One will help you decide. You'll also enjoy our unique color and pattern quizzes that will help you see your decorating choices in a fresh—and totally personal—light. Throughout the book, we help you apply those newfound thoughts to create the most comfortable and livable rooms you have ever known.

Whether you're planning a whole room or simply looking for ways to freshen what you already have with a few pillows or bright new color and pattern on the walls, this book will be with you every step of the way. The first step is the easiest: Settle back, relax, and enjoy the hundreds of color photos. Then begin planning your own great projects. As you use this book to help you decorate in the coming months, let us hear from you. Your feedback will help us plan future products and books to serve *your* needs.

Christiane Michaels

President, Waverly®

6 **know yourself.** know your style. know your home.

40 past perfect   86 town&country

224 **your workroom.** projects and tips.

contents

126 modern living   176 beautiful things

235 resources   239 index

know yourself

inspirations

hat do you want your home to be? A safe, comfortable nest for raising children? A quiet haven for refreshing your spirit? A lively social center for crowds of family and friends? Perhaps it's all of these at different times of the day, the year, or even your stage in life. Decorating is all about letting your home reflect who you are—your interests, your attitudes, your personality. It's about creating an environment that's nurturing, relaxing, and welcoming for you and your family. That's why decorating is so personal.

Making your house a place you love to come home to starts with identifying how you and your family live in your rooms. If you have energetic children and large dogs with sofa privileges, you'll probably be happier with a slipcovered, overstuffed sofa and a butcher-block coffee table than with a camelback settee and a Queen Anne tea table.

To help you explore your decorating preferences, take the lifestyle quiz on the following pages. Relax and have fun with it—there aren't any right answers, except what's right for you.

What's your style?

For each question, choose the answer that best reflects your preferences. If none of the answers seems exactly right, choose the one that's closest. Then use the analysis starting on page 13 to bring home some fresh insights.

1. Friends are treating you to a birthday getaway weekend at the bed-and-breakfast of your choice. You choose:

a. A seaside Victorian with a wraparound porch for watching the sunset

b. The faithfully restored turn-of-the-century mansion of an eccentric English collector

c. A small midtown hotel within walking distance of art galleries, antiques stores, and thrift shops

d. A colonial-era clapboard that features garden walks of its historic environs

2. At a dinner party, if you could switch place cards and sit next to anyone past or present, who would it be?

a. Queen Victoria

b. Architect Frank Lloyd Wright

c. Actor Leonardo diCaprio

d. English gardener Gertrude Jekyll

3. For which book would you attend a book-signing party at the neighborhood bookstore?

a. *England's Cotswold Cottages*

b. *Confessions of a Wine Connoisseur*

c. *Climbing Mount Everest*

d. *French Renaissance Furniture Makers*

4. If you could turn back time and shop for a piece of design history, which would you choose?

a. The late 1800s for a Victorian wicker rocking chair

b. The 1840s for a Biedermeier-style library table

c. The 1930s for vintage table linens and advertising art

d. The late 1700s for a set of Thomas Sheraton's dining chairs

5. You've had this must-see museum event on your calendar for weeks:

Is this your style?

a. "A Day in the Country" exhibit
   of Impressionist painters
b. "The Art and Artifacts of Pompeii"
c. "American Folk Art Furniture"
d. "English Portraits from the
   18th Century"

6. Your dream car would be:
   a. A Miata convertible
   b. A Land Rover
   c. A new VW bug
   d. A Ford Explorer

Is this your style?

7. One house-for-sale ad in the newspaper's real estate section has you on your feet and out the door for a firsthand look. It's for:
   a. The Victorian Lady bed-and-breakfast that's gone
      out of business
   b. A renovated brownstone
   c. A "fixer-upper" barn
   d. A late-1800s carriage house

8. Your favorite spot for at-home relaxing is:
   a. A wicker chaise longue on the porch
   b. An overstuffed chair in the den with a city skyline view
   c. A slipcovered love seat in front of your
      entertainment center
   d. A wing chair in the living room, overlooking the garden

9. Your bedroom lacks character so you decide to:
   a. Embellish built-in cabinetry with stenciling
   b. Create a wainscoting effect with a
      wallcovering border
   c. Paint the walls crisp white and dress the bed
      in pretty print fabrics
   d. Hang lace panels from the ceiling at the head
      of the bed to suggest a half-canopy

10. You prefer to dress your home's windows in:
   a. Simple draperies with
      valances and shades in
      coordinating fabrics
   b. Rich fabrics swagged over
      interesting hardware and
      puddled on the floor
   c. Crisp Roman shades or white
      miniblinds
   d. Formal swags and jabots with
      luxurious fringe trims

11. When guests are due, your favorite floral arrangement for the dining table is:
   a. Mixed wildflowers in a Depression-glass vase or
      hammered aluminum pitcher
   b. Corkscrew willow and birds-of-paradise in a
      bronze container
   c. Gerbera daisies in sea-glass vases
   d. Cabbage roses in a Waterford bowl

12. Among some of the treasures you display on your mantel are:
   a. Your grandfather's wooden tea caddy
   b. Moroccan bone-inlaid box and a model of a sailing ship
   c. Flea market pottery and framed movie stills from the 1940s
   d. A landscape painting of the English countryside

13. For that special dinner party, you pull out the stops and set the table with:
   a. Willowware plates and Grandmother's silverware
   b. Formal gilt-edged plates and fine crystal
   c. Handcrafted pottery plates and mismatched
      champagne flutes from the flea market
   d. Heirloom bone china plates and silver serving pieces

14. In the living room, you'd like to corral entertainment gear in:
   a. An old corner cupboard
   b. Built-ins with raised-panel doors
   c. A reproduction pie safe
   d. A French armoire

15. Suppose you're checking out antiques and secondhand shops just opened in a restored warehouse. The store you can't resist stopping at first is:
   a. Queen Anne's Lace, an inviting collection of old quilts and lace, weathered-looking cottage-style furniture, fragrant potpourris and candles, and romantic antiques
   b. Call of the Wild, an exciting assortment of imported treasures from exotic places, along with animal-print pillows and accessories and antiques related to exploration and travel
   c. Uncommon Treasures, an eclectic collection of flea market finds, contemporary crafts, and stylish metal furniture and decorative accessories
   d. The Palace Attic, a bit of the British Isles transported to America, with antique and reproduction English furniture, needlepoint pillows, tole-painted accessories, and Chinese porcelain

16. For you, the perfect living room seating would be:
   a. An 1800s pine settee you can dress up with pillows and cushions
   b. A long, cushy traditional-style sofa
   c. A love seat to pair with 1930s club chairs
   d. A classic camelback sofa upholstered in elegant damask

Is this your style?

17. You'd browse an architectural salvage shop for:
   a. A weathered garden gate
   b. Architectural fragments to use as sculpture
   c. Unusual finials for drapery rods
   d. Gilded sconces or wall brackets

18. If you could add outdoor living space, it would be:
   a. A gazebo with gingerbread trim
   b. A balcony off the bedroom
   c. A terrace of salvaged bricks
   d. A rose-covered arbor and patio

19. The local university is sponsoring a decorative arts lecture series. You choose the seminar on:
   a. 19th-century crockery from the American South
   b. Asian ceramics
   c. 20th-century art pottery
   d. Wedgwood

20. When you visit friends' homes, what's the one thing that makes their rooms inviting and interesting?
   a. Plenty of sink-in seating and a put-your-feet-up ottoman
   b. Intriguing collections artfully displayed
   c. Mismatched vintage furniture and whimsical accents
   d. Antiques and family photos that evoke a sense of history

21. If you had the time and space, how would your garden grow?
   a. A lush cottage garden just steps from the back door
   b. Patio containers of bright-hued annuals and rose-tree topiaries
   c. A mini-meadow of wildflowers in the backyard
   d. Formal flower beds outlined with low boxwood hedges

22. You're looking for the perfect bed for the guest room, so you would buy:

    a. A twin-size sleigh bed that can double as seating

    b. An antique iron bed with gilded medallions

    c. Fabric to upholster the headboard on a hand-me-down bed

    d. A bed with traditional mahogany headboard and footboard

23. On a free weekend when you can treat yourself to a favorite pursuit, you are likely to be:

    a. Working on the family genealogy

    b. Browsing an antiquarian bookstore

    c. Up to your elbows in do-it-yourself projects

    d. Pruning your roses

24. In your decorating "library," one of your favorite books is on:

    a. Key West's Victorian cottages

    b. Renovating a vineyard home in Tuscany

    c. America's best-known flea markets

    d. The homes of Provence

25. That dream vacation you've been planning forever would find you:

    a. Exploring the historic seaside villages of New England

    b. On a wine-tasting tour of Italy

    c. Trekking the Appalachian Trail

    d. Touring the great gardens of England

26. You've taken the collector's vow to resist temptation, but you can't when you see:

    a. Four English botanical prints in original weathered frames

    b. A matched set of gilded compotes on marble pedestals

    c. A 1940s tomato-shaped ceramic teapot

    d. A bronze cupid sculpture that once graced a garden

27. What's your ideal view?

    a. A pond framed by a rose-covered arbor

    b. The city skyline at night

    c. A birch forest and mountains beyond the deck

    d. A historic harbor dotted with sailboats

28. Which statement describes what you'd like others to say about your decorating style?

    a. You have a fresh take on the past.

    b. You're discriminating and adventuresome.

    c. You don't take yourself too seriously.

    d. You like to put down roots.

Analyzing the results

This is a quiz you can't fail because there are no right or wrong answers—only answers that are right for you. Have fun trying on the results to see which of the following styles suits you best.

    If you chose A most often, you're drawn to a Past Perfect collection of vintage looks that can range in inspiration from American country to Victorian and Scandinavian. You treasure vintage furniture, accessories, and collections, and you enjoy displaying them to surround yourself with nostalgic references to the past. Old-fashioned comfort is your decorating priority. Cottage-style pieces and finds from the Victorian era

Is this your style?

are sure to catch your eye when you're browsing shops and flea markets, but you choose judiciously because you prefer cleaner, airier spaces than the country styles of the 1970s and 1980s. You like to keep things fresh and casual, decorating in a soft, mellow color palette and mixing a new bouquet of Victorian- or Scandinavian-inspired florals with old quilts and textiles.

If you chose B most often, a sophisticated Town and Country look may be for you. Your rooms can be comfortably formal or informal, but they're sure to have a refined, sophisticated air. You like to imbue your home with classic elegance, blending historical motifs drawn from art and architecture, luxurious fabrics, and rich colors; but you easily mix these with contemporary pieces

with strong, bold lines for an eclectic look. No matter where your travels take you, you can spot the artful and unusual object and find just the right place for it at home. You enjoy accessorizing your classic furnishings with mementos, art, and sculpture that can range from gilt-framed paintings to exotic treasures.

If you chose C most often, you have an affinity for a fresh, lighthearted Modern Living style. You're not into stark minimalism, but neither do you want to be smothered by pattern and clutter. Bright, bold colors make you happy, and you give yourself visual and psychological room to breathe by choosing graphic checks and stripes and lively prints with airy backgrounds. Flea market finds—wearing their original paint—and family hand-me-downs give your

A. past perfect   B. town&country

rooms an easygoing comfort and charm. But because you always find a place for sentimental and whimsical accessories, yours is a look that's contemporary and transitional.

If you chose D most often, you're a romantic traditionalist attracted to Beautiful Things. Gracious living means surrounding yourself with 18th-century English and French classics, blending rich woods and overstuffed seating into high-comfort rooms that are pretty and fresh, never stuffy. Searching though antiques shops, you look for furniture in established styles that imparts a sense of history and for accessories with the same enduring appeal—such as needlepoint pillows and floral-motif textiles. The English garden inspires your wallpapers and the fabrics you choose for upholstery and window treatments.

If your answers don't place you clearly in any one group, you're probably eclectic in your tastes, comfortably mixing and matching styles according to your mood or the demands of the space. In fact, lifestyles are subjective and personal, not set in stone; and just because you prefer one style for your living room does not mean you have to stay with that style throughout your home. You may want to cook and entertain in a kitchen that's crisp, bright, and friendly in the Modern Living mode, but retire for the evening to a bedroom that's pure Past Perfect, lavishly swagged and draped in soft florals and lace. Decorating is all about creating spaces that reflect who you are and that express your definition of comfort.

c. modern living   d. beautiful things

What's your hue?

Color is the most powerful tool you have for creating a mood. You're energized every morning when you step into your citrus-hued bathroom and lulled to sleep by your bedroom's sky blue walls.

but everyone's emotional response to color is different, and you know your friend's red, black, and white kitchen just isn't for you. By taking a thoughtful approach to selecting colors for your home, you can customize your environment so you're happier, more relaxed, and even, some experts say, healthier. Start your color quest by picturing the following everyday objects. In the blank spaces, jot down the feelings you associate with the color of each one.

Ripe tomatoes _____
Cotton candy _____
Buttercups in bloom _____
An ebony sculpture _____
Paperwhite narcissus _____
A swimming pool _____
Autumn leaves _____
Fresh nutmeg _____
A manicured lawn _____
An amethyst ring _____

The feelings and memories these items bring to mind affect the way you respond to the colors most commonly linked to them. If the thought of a swimming pool makes you feel relaxed and cool, for example, you probably will feel the same way if you use aqua or clear blue in a room. If, on the other hand, cotton candy reminds you of the time you overindulged at the fair, pastel pink may be too sticky sweet for you.

Your color "EQ" (Emotional Quotient) may relate broadly to your style preferences—Past Perfect, for example, calls for soft, aged colors rather than bold, bright ones—but you can put your favorite colors to work in any style category. For more insights into which colors may be just right for your home, take the following quiz, choosing the answers that are closest to your tastes. See page 18 for the results.

1. Where do you go when you want to relax?
   a. The museum to view a contemporary art exhibit
   b. The woods for an afternoon hike
   c. The beach for early-morning shell collecting

2. When your "inner child" needs a just-for-fun field trip, you head for:
  a. The toy store   b. The water park   c. The zoo

3. Friends tease about your "weekend uniform." It's a:
  a. Red sweatshirt and jeans
  b. Chambray shirt and jeans
  c. Cream-color cable-knit sweater and jeans

4. If your coworkers sent you a getwell present from the garden, what would cheer you up the most?
  a. Pale pink and yellow Peace roses
  b. A small ficus tree
  c. Lily-of-the-valley

5. The predominant color in your favorite artwork is:
  a. Peach   b. Sage   c. Brown

6. If you were an herb or spice, you'd be:
  a. Saffron   b. Basil   c. Cinnamon

7. You must paint your formal dining room walls one of the following colors; which would you choose to make it more intimate?

a.    b.    c.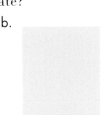

8. Your new car will be:
  a. Canary   b. Periwinkle   c. Charcoal

9. Your cookware is:
  a. Orange enamelware
  b. Blue spatterware from the flea market
  c. Stainless steel

10. On a trip to the tropics, you can't resist buying:
  a. A citrus-print bikini
  b. A watercolor painting of a seascape
  c. Pale beige handwoven baskets

11. Friends are coming for a theme brunch; you set the table with:
  a. Pottery on a Mexican serape
  b. Blue Willow china on a flower-garden quilt
  c. White plates on a natural linen runner

12. The brightest remodeling idea you've had is adding a:
  a. Fireplace in the living room
  b. Greenhouse/sitting room off the master bedroom
  c. Clerestory windows in the bath

13. Friends describe your living room as "The Tunnel." Which paint colors would you use to change that effect?
  a. Deep red on the end walls and rosy white on the side walls
  b. Hunter green on the end walls and pale green on the side walls
  c. Cocoa brown on the end walls and blush beige on the side walls

14. In a frivolous moment, you let a friend coax you into a vintage-clothing store, where you unexpectedly buy a:
  a. Bandanna-print sun hat
  b. Purple velvet beret
  c. Black satin top hat

15. Your bedroom ceiling is boring, so you:
  a. Paint it the same goldenrod yellow as the walls
  b. Paint a faux sky with fluffy clouds
  c. Drape it in muslin like a circus tent

16. They're remodeling at the office, and your boss asks you which colors would make you more productive. You say:

   a. Shades of red and yellow

   b. Shades of blue and green

   c. Black, white, and gray

17. In your jewelry box, your favorite ring is:

   a. Ruby   b. Turquoise   c. Opal

18. On a garden tour, you're enchanted by:

   a. A border of Oriental poppies

   b. Indigo pansies in a window box

   c. An elaborate rock garden

19. The neighborhood bistro is your favorite as much for the decor as for the food. It's:

   a. "Taste of Provence," with sunny-colored linens and terra-cotta accents

   b. "The Garden Gate," a greenhouse with lace-covered tables

   c. "Extra" with newspaper-print tablecloths and front-page wallcovering

20. At the flea market, you can't believe you were lucky enough to find:

   a. An orange Fiestaware bowl

   b. A tea-dyed floral pillow

   c. Enough old muslin to make kitchen curtains

21. For a summery slipcover for the sofa, you'd choose fabric in:

   a. Butter yellow chintz

   b. Mint green floral miniprint

   c. Natural canvas

A. WARM COLORS

Analyzing the results

Add up the number of answers you have in each letter category. If you have more A answers, you prefer warm, active colors; if more B answers, you lean toward cool, passive colors; and if more C answers, you're drawn to calm, neutral colors.

   A. Warm Colors. You love high-energy hues such as reds, oranges, yellows, and pinks. Anywhere the action is—dining, living, or family rooms—you like these activating colors. Even if you cool things down a bit elsewhere, your entry always has a punch of warm color.

   Red purifies, unifies, and enlivens other colors. It animates and excites, and depending on the tone or intensity of the hue, it can suggest cozy warmth or vigorous health. With red walls, the den where the

B. COOL COLORS   C. NEUTRAL COLORS

family gathers couldn't be cozier, and in the dining room, red walls stimulate appetites and conversation. Orange refreshes, balances, and encourages emotional growth. As a color for interiors, true orange can be brash and loud, a difficult color to live with in large quantities. Tints and tones, however, such as peach, melon, coral, persimmon, and pumpkin, introduce the warmth of orange in a quieter way. Yellow cheers and lifts the spirit; like red, it can stimulate appetites and conversation. Pink promotes affability and affection.

B. Cool Colors. Shades and tints of blues, greens, and purples create a soothing, relaxing atmosphere and link interior spaces to the outdoors. Bedrooms, living rooms, spas, or porches in these colors demand only that you rest and renew your

spirit. Blue promotes concentration and serenity; it comforts and is said to draw out intuition. Green stabilizes the emotions and symbolizes a down-to-earth attitude. Purple strengthens resolve and encourages independence.

C. Neutral Colors. These easygoing colors—black, brown, white, gray, beige, and taupe—are easy on the eye and easy to incorporate into decorating schemes. Neutrals let you keep your options open if you're unwilling to commit to color. Black warms things up and increases your energy. Brown empowers and can symbolize passion. White refreshes the spirit and promotes tranquillity.

If your answers were evenly divided among the categories, include warm and cool colors throughout your home and use congenial neutrals to link them.

Cool colors: soft and intense

Love cool colors? As these fabric swatches show, you can choose low- or high-intensity versions of the same color to create entirely different moods.

Both of these cool-color palettes are based on blue, but the one on *page 20* is soft, while the one on this page is intense. The rooms shown use different fabrics and wallpapers to make the same point. Note that in each room, a touch of a warm color (yellow in the soft scheme, red in the intense) is included to create a satisfyingly balanced scheme.

Warm colors: soft and intense

Prefer warm colors? Your choices don't stop there. As these swatches and photos show, you can choose muted or clear, bright or bold.

The rosy pink fabrics on *page 22* are warm and soft but muted, creating a vintage feeling. The pastel pink in the bedroom on *page 22* is also soft but clear, giving an airy, delicate effect. Intense warm colors can be bright, like the yellow fabrics *at left*, creating an energetic, cheerful mood. Or they can be bold, as in the living room *below*, where the high-intensity red creates a cozy warmth.

Neutral colors: warm and cool

Neutrals may be warm or cool. A room decorated entirely in cool neutrals may feel too chilly, so consider heating it up with touches of a warm neutral.

To check the temperature of a neutral color, hold a piece of jewelry against it: Silver draws out the icy tones of cool neutrals like those on this page, while gold picks up the heat in warm ones like those on *page 24*. To anchor a cool-neutral scheme, include a dose of a warm neutral, such as the chocolate brown and the print at *left*. With warm neutrals, choose a variety of textures to keep the room visually interesting.

The color wheel

All colors may live happily together in nature, but indoors most people are more comfortable with an orderly scheme of a few colors. To learn how to assemble a satisfying combination of hues, start with the color wheel.

You've narrowed your color choices and identified the intensity that will create the mood you want. Now what? One way to develop a color scheme is to use the color wheel, which shows how colors relate to each other. About half of the wheel consists of the warm colors—the yellows and reds. The blues, greens, and violets make up the cool colors. Artists use a wheel with pie-shaped wedges of pure hues to guide them in mixing colors, but your choices for home decorating are broader than such a wheel suggests. That's why we made this color wheel oval shaped, using paint colors like those you'll find in the real world of decorating.

To build a color scheme, you can start with your favorite color and jump across the wheel to the opposite side to find its complement. Or start with one color and choose several of its adjoining neighbors to create an analogous scheme. If you like more variety, choose any three colors that are equally spaced on the wheel for a triadic scheme. (See *pages 28–29* for color combination examples.) These combinations work with tints or shades as well as with the pure colors. As a rule, keep the intensities of the colors in the same range, either all soft or all intense; this generally yields the most harmonious effect.

Creating color schemes

Once you've chosen a color you love, use the color wheel to help you select compatible colors. Basic schemes include complementary, analogous, monochromatic, and triadic.

Complementary schemes pair two colors that lie opposite each other on the color wheel. Complements intensify each other—red looks more vibrant when paired with green; yellow is more satisfying when balanced by a dose of purple or its neighbor, blue. Choose any two or three neighbors on the wheel and you have an analogous color scheme. This palette is easy on the eye because all of the colors are related. For the most satisfying effect in a room, let one color dominate and cast the other two in supporting roles. Monochromatic schemes use one color or a neutral in a range of tints and shades. (Tints are made by adding white to a color; shades are made by adding black or the complementary color.) Triadic schemes pull together three hues that are equally spaced on the wheel: red, yellow, and blue, for example, or peach, sage, and violet. As you build your color scheme, remember that the degree of contrast between hues will affect the room's feeling. High contrast juxtaposes a very dark color with a very light one. This creates an active feeling because your eye dances from one color to the next. A low-contrast mix combines all-dark or all-light colors. Low-contrast schemes are easy to live with because the tones are more even, creating a tranquil effect.

MONOCHROMATIC

TRIADIC

What's your pattern?

Once you've chosen the colors you want to live with, think about layering on pattern and texture. Take this quiz, then turn to pages 32 and 33 to see which patterns speak your language.

1. With this toile wallcovering, which fabric in row 1 *opposite* would you choose for the bedroom's duvet and drapes?

2. You've got just the spot in the living room for a flea market find—a carved wood armchair—so you would:
   a. Give it a natural finish and hunter green plaid upholstery
   b. Give it a cherry stain and Indian-inspired tree-of-life upholstery
   c. Give it an antiqued white finish and rose-trellis print upholstery
   d. Paint it white and upholster it with natural linen

3. Your sofa is slipcovered in this floral print. Which fabric in row 2 *opposite* would you choose to upholster an armchair in the same room?

4. You want to use Grandmother's blue-and-white star quilt as a table topper in the garden room. Which fabric in row 3 *opposite* would you choose for the love seat?

5. In your closet, the patterned piece of apparel you wear most often is a:
   a. Buffalo-plaid shirt
   b. Paisley scarf
   c. Denim shirt embroidered with flowers
   d. Tweed jacket

6. You want to put your wood-paneled den in an English country home mood. Which fabric in row 4 *opposite* do you choose for the fireside wing chair?

7. To jazz up your dining room's painted walls, you'd choose a wallpaper border patterned with:
   a. Windowpane checks
   b. A paisley print
   c. Botanical prints
   d. A faux-marble cornice design

QUESTION 1

a.

b.

c.

d.

QUESTION 3

a.

b.

c.

d.

QUESTION 4

a.

b.

c.

d.

QUESTION 6

a.

b.

c.

d.

Analyzing the results

Now tally your answers to see which patterns make you feel at home. If you have more A answers, check out checks and stripes; more B answers, toiles and motifs (that is, repeat patterns of any kind); more C answers, floral prints; and more D answers, fabrics whose pattern comes from their textures rather than a woven-in or printed design.

If you're drawn to plaids, stripes, and checks, you define visual comfort in terms of order, regularity, neatness, and restraint. These geometric patterns supply a clean simplicity and a sense of structure, precision, and order. As the dominant motif in a room, they can be prim or playful, depending on the width of the stripe or the size of the check and the colors they're worked in. Wide, high-contrast stripes, for example, can make you feel as if you're in a circus tent, while narrow, tone-on-tone stripes suggest a dignified formality. Vertical stripes tease the eye upward, making the ceiling seem higher.

Checks and plaids are equally versatile. A large check in cream and taupe silk is contemporary but elegant on a Louis XV chair,

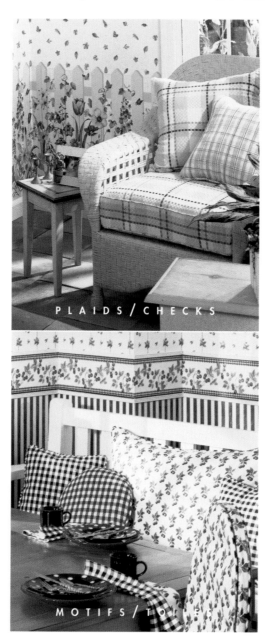

PLAIDS / CHECKS

MOTIFS / TOILES

while a tiny red-and-white check suits the country simplicity of a ladder-back chair. Used as accent patterns, checks, plaids, and stripes can rein in exuberant florals and tone them down. If you're combining several check or plaid fabrics, link them with color and vary the scale; combining small, medium, and large checks or plaids provides the best visual mix.

If you're drawn to motifs and toiles, you define visual comfort in terms of repetition, balance, and order. Toiles, which chronicle scenes from everyday life or depict the activities of mythological characters, have a narrative quality. Surrounding yourself with these pictorial patterns suggests a lively interest in human affairs and in stories about people and their lives. Toile is a high-impact pattern; it can be intimidating to work with but can deliver beautiful results, especially when used as a wall-covering or on large furnishings such as sofas, draperies, and bed dressings.

Motifs include any repeat pattern, from geometrics such as scrolls, dots, and diamonds, to representational designs, such as fruit, shells, and cherubs. Because the pattern repeats, it has a geometric quality that serves the same orderly function as checks and stripes in a room full of florals. But the nature of the motif also determines its impact in a room. A grid of fleurs-de-lis is formal and elegant, while polka dots or bees are playful.

If you're primarily drawn to florals, you're a romantic at heart, whatever your decorating personality. Flowers are such an enduring and adaptable motif that you'll find them in fabrics and wallpapers for every lifestyle. Exuberant bouquets of multi-hued flowers generally suit a Beautiful Things look, while grids of blossoms with a hand-painted quality suggest a Modern Living feeling. Stylized florals inspired by Asian or Indian art have a formal, classic quality that suits the sophisticated Town and Country style. Florals work well in any role, from wallcoverings and upholstery to accents and wallcovering borders. You can mix florals easily, provided you vary the scale, choosing small, medium, and large prints, and link them with color. Let one floral dominate to anchor the mix.

If you prefer textures over patterns, subtlety is your signature. You want warm, comfortable

FLORALS

TEXTURES

rooms without a lot of pattern, so you stick to the classic weaves that create interest when light bounces off them. Textured fabrics invite you to touch them, and since they appeal to the visual and tactile senses, they can be powerful mood-setters. Airy organdy, filmy cottons, and crisp linens are breezy and summer-fresh; silky chenille and felted wool are as snuggly as a warm sweater; velvets, shiny silks, and taffeta moiré are elegant and luxurious.

Use contrast to keep a textural palette interesting, but make sure the textures have something in common, too. A shiny silk damask will look out of place paired with a dull-finish woven cotton, but a nubby raw silk will look just right. In the photo *at left*, velvet pillows and pillow shams offer touchable texture; the chenille check on the bolster in the right corner combines woven pattern with texture.

Take advantage of the textural possibilities of trims, too. Shiny or lustrous fringe and tassels enhance the rich effect of velvets, damasks, and formal-looking fabrics, while matte-finish cotton trims complement fabrics with a dull finish or coarse, woven texture.

Putting it all together

You know which colors evoke the mood you want to create and you've identified the patterns you love. Now put them all together.

the easiest way to begin is to find a fabric you love that combines your color and pattern preferences. It will be your "signature print." If it's just one color plus white, use the color wheel to help you choose coordinating colors that will create the look you want. If it's a multicolor print, choose one or two secondary colors from the print to accent the dominant hue. As a rule, use the dominant hue on as much as two-thirds of the available area to anchor the room visually. Use the secondary colors to accent your main theme. In the room *at right*, for example, the green damask on the sofa and ottoman draws out the background color in the floral panel between the windows; the green-and-purple stripe on the armchairs acts as a secondary accent.

How do you decide where to use each pattern? Its scale will suggest its best use. A large-scale floral, for example, will show to advantage on draperies or a sofa, but its impact could be lost on a small side chair. One approach is to use your signature print on about two-thirds of the room's area, such as on a pair of upholstered chairs and at the windows. Use a coordinate on an ottoman and pillows, and skirt decorator tables with

Are you passionate about pattern? Wrap the room in it, *right*, by distributing several favorite patterns evenly around the space. To call attention to one area of the room, such as the sofa, *page 35*, concentrate your dominant pattern there. For balance, repeat a pattern three times.

a third print. Be sure to include a solid, perhaps on the sofa, to give the eye a place to rest.

Another approach is to make sure you use each pattern at least three times. For example, use the same signature-print floral on the draperies and sofa. Use color-coordinated checks and smaller florals on pillows, upholstered chairs, and table skirts. Study the photos in this book for ideas on ways to distribute patterns around the room and choose the ones that appeal to you most. Let these guide you in deciding how to use the patterns you've chosen.

In general, plan to distribute patterns evenly so they feel balanced. The exception: If you want to focus attention on one area, cluster the pattern to pull the eye to that spot. Take care to balance it visually with something equally weighty, such as a fireplace or a large piece of furniture.

To create a feeling of unity and flow through your home (or through the living areas that connect to one another visually), use color as the thread that ties areas together. You can mix and match the same palette of fabrics for all rooms, varying the way you use them from one room to the next. A plaid on the living room sofa, for example, can dress the windows in the dining room. Or choose different fabrics in harmonizing colors to create variations on a theme from room to room. (For examples, see *pages 90–93, 130–35,* and *180–87.*)

Pick a pattern, pick a mood

Any print can lend itself to a variety of decorating styles, depending on the fabrics you choose to go with it. These examples show how to start with a floral, a stripe, or a check and create different moods with each.

LEFT: If you start with a
Modern Living stripe, pair it
with bold complementary
checks and a gridded print for
a spirited look. Or use white
and a sheer with a green motif
for a quietly monochromatic
palette. For a serene but
cheerful analogous color
scheme, choose checks and
floral stripes in blue and green.

PAGE 36: Starting with a floral, create
a formal English look in the Beautiful
Things style by partnering the print with
refined, textured solids: two neutrals,
one with a slubbed silk texture and one
with a bouclé weave. Add a paprika
red for a strong accent. Create a Past
Perfect mood like that suggested by the
room on *page 36* with a soft, neutral ivy
print and coordinating neutrals in solids
and a plaid. The neutrals emphasize the
faded quality of the signature floral.
To evoke a Town and Country look, use
a selection of red or warm-neutral
checks, stripes, and solids in coarse or
linenlike textures.

If a plaid is your starting point, evoke the "country" part of Town and Country with red checks and solids, a small-scale floral, and a black-background floral. For a Past Perfect look, choose a soft floral and a muted stripe with a darker solid for emphasis. Or suggest a country-French feeling with prints and stripes that repeat the two colors in the plaid. Mix large, medium, and small prints and stripes for interest.

What's your style? If you love the calm, restful effect of soft, subdued colors, choose pastels and muted tints to go with your signature floral. If you prefer the more energetic, active look of strong color and high contrast, pick out the floral's darker colors with solids and coordinating stripes. Still feel timid? Collections of prints in coordinating colors make mixing and matching easy.

inspirations past perfect

Vintage, nostalgic, aged, mellow. Objects and surfaces with a timeworn look can connect our rooms—and spirits—to the past as we move into the future. Tarnished metal chairs and wooden cabinets covered in layers of peeling paint speak of years of use; mix-and-match china, plain pine furniture, and old paintings darkened with age suggest an accumulation of family heirlooms whose value is more sentimental than monetary. Fabrics that have a tea-stained look or are printed in soft, muted colors convey the impression of having been aged by time. Together the objects and the fabrics give a room a sense of being rooted in the past, filled with family or personal history and a distinctive spirit acquired through being loved and lived with. Vintage-inspired fabrics can evoke a casual atmosphere that invites you to sit back and put your feet up. Or, on more traditional furnishings, they suggest country style with a pedigree—croquet on the lawn and afternoon tea.

Garden influences

Guided by images of the cottage gardens and porches of the past, the owner of this home created rooms to relax in. Come in for a tour and a bouquet of ideas designed to refresh any home with back-roads charm.

When a decorating scheme has its roots in the garden, working from the outside in is the natural thing to do. In fact, if your spirit naturally gravitates toward the colors, materials, and textures of the outdoors, why not begin a whole house redecorating project on the porch as this homeowner did? Wicker or rattan plus a mix of garden accessories make easy starting points. But what about color? To choose your porch palette, ask yourself: Do you find cool colors refreshing—or depressing? Do you feel that warm colors are energizing—or irritating? Also, consider your room's natural light; if windows face south or west, you may want some cool blues or greens to counteract excessive sunlight. On the other hand, consider a warmer palette to add sunny ambience to a north-facing

Wicker seating pieces, floral fabrics, and green plants lay the foundation for this vintage-style porch scheme. It's the aged accessories with their timeworn finishes that give this space its Past Perfect personality.

space that receives little direct sunlight. Here, dominant greens create cool comfort all summer long, while red and pink accents add welcome warmth. Love the look? Step back now and see how garden accents and colors work together to create this inviting gathering spot. A vintage classic, wicker offers a nostalgic nod to the past, but its perennial popularity also stems from the easygoing attitude it imparts to any space. Here, the rugged texture of wicker seating pieces creates a casual look that's just right for sitting down with a book or visiting with friends. Clad in durable cotton, floral and striped cushions and pillows bring garden colors and motifs indoors. When rain clouds threaten, the cushions easily stow away inside.

Naturally refreshing, a palette of green soothes modern spirits with the cool calm of springtime meadows and wooded glens.

layering of textures helps to give this porch its mellow, evolved-over-time appearance. Recast as a display shelf, an old stepladder features paint that's peeling away to reveal weathered wood. Beneath it, an aging tin double boiler serves as a planter. Weathered terra-cotta pots and glossy antique crocks add more texture and nostalgia to the setting.

The romance continues in the background, where flowing white sheers, layered over matchstick blinds, not only soften the porch's hard edges

Instead of taking themselves seriously, birdhouses, watering cans, and garden boots serve as lighthearted "sculpture." An old wooden chair with a missing seat becomes a witty planter when a friendly mixing bowl drops in to fill the void.

47

but also add a decidedly romantic "grand-ma's house" touch. Like the curtains, a natural sisal rug brightens the setting, putting a border of flowers underfoot while offering airy counterpoint to the earthy textures, brown wicker, and dark greens.

he porch's fresh outdoor spirit flows into adjacent living spaces, providing these garden-loving homeowners with an alfresco-style retreat to enjoy year-round. Although the garden feeling connects the porch and living room, indoors the mood softens, becoming more refined than rustic. Celestial blue walls and crisp white shutters create a breezy backdrop for this cottage-garden scheme. With their gathered skirts and a variety of new and collectible pillows, the rolled-arm seating pieces lend a cottage look, but it's the floral fabrics themselves that bring the garden inside. Just as flowers mix in a meadow, disparate blooms gather on the sofa, chair, and ottoman. Twiggy tables, white wicker, and green plants also bring the outdoors in.

If your idea of perfection is a cottage garden from the past, bring the feeling indoors with blooming fabrics and a mix of wicker and twiggy accents.

Evoking sky and clouds, light blue walls and crisp white trim give the living room its airy, outdoor style. Rolled-arm seating pieces suggest the comforts of the past—a feeling underscored by the muted colors of the new slipcovers.

As if yellowed by time, off-white, "tea-stained" backgrounds give new fabrics a coveted, aged look. Flea market pillows, like the fringed example on the chair, *left,* add more antique ambience. Mixing several fabrics on one furniture piece—in this case on newly sewn slipcovers, *right*—not only underscores the "collected" look that's vital to Past Perfect schemes, but also creates the chance to save by using small amounts of expensive fabrics. A more costly toile de Jouy from a designer line covers just the top of the seat cushion and ottoman, while less expensive yardage makes up the rest. For added charm, a checked fabric covers the cording that outlines each piece.

For cottage style, consider a new slipcover that mixes several fabrics, all in muted garden hues. The final touch? Gathered skirts that recall the charm of grandma's aprons.

Layering collections

Well-loved accessories form the heart and soul of Past Perfect rooms. Whether they're new or old, your special treasures, gathered over time, imbue any vintage setting with one-of-a-kind personality.

Pedigree matters less than personality when you're collecting objects for a Past Perfect room. Let a favorite fabric, whether beautifully flowered or jauntily checked, set the color scheme. Then start scouting flea markets, grandma's attic, and new boutiques for pieces that will accent your style. The creativity is in the recasting of objects. An old tin becomes a vase. A bowl holds a grouping of candles. Yesterday's outdoor bench moves into the living room as a nostalgic coffee table. The fun, of course, lies in the decorating process as much as in the finished room. The only rule: Find a theme or a mood and stick with it. If you're unsure of the look you want, clip photos of rooms you love from magazines. When you have a dozen or more, look for what they have in common. Chances are that some of the same colors, materials, or feelings will link the clippings.

Ah-h-h-h...Generously stuffed seat cushions and pillows help an old wicker settee soothe modern spirits—and bodies. Rising above the frame of the sofa itself, the back pillows create irresistible, settle-back ease.

Even a city apartment or a suburban tract house can offer the charm of the past when nostalgic furniture, fabrics, and accessories come to play.

pirited, yet nostalgic, the cottage style of this irresistible living room belies its modern city location. Best of all, this easygoing design approach provides an antique look on a flea market budget. The starting point? Easy to mix (and easy to *love*) wicker seating pieces. Shop for new pieces, as well as flea market finds, testing for durability by sitting on the piece and by standing and pushing down on the arms. If the piece gives too much under your weight, keep shopping. Next, choose new fabrics to pull your scheme together. Plump cushions covered in bold florals set a mood that's nostalgic yet light enough to keep small spaces from closing in. For a colorful accent, paint a wicker chair a contrasting color. Here, an old rocker dresses in a new coat of sage green paint.

Create a fabric focal point—and block out a less-than-vintage city or suburban view—with this simple curtain. Stitched together, flat fabric panels in contrasting stripes and checks loop back to create a graceful swirl. For more privacy and light control, add miniblinds or shutters.

a s you learned in the quiz on pages 10–15, depending on the fabrics and accessories you choose, Past Perfect rooms can range from American country and Victorian to European. The looks, whether light and airy or dark and cozy, depend on your own taste and personality. In contrast to the American farmhouse feeling of the living room on *page 55*, the room here welcomes friends and family with snug warmth and a hint of European traditions. Richly colored fabrics and darker woods set the mellow scene. The lush, muted floral of the sofa repeats at the windows in long curtain panels that hang like tapestries from black metal rods. Small windows gain height and grandeur when framed with a simple floor-to-ceiling window treatment, which carries the eye upward for a room-heightening effect. Against this backdrop, the accessories lend old-world character. Aging oil paintings, timeworn leather-bound books, and a tin trunk ground the setting in the past.

Let one wall showcase your Past Perfect treasures. The tricks? Move a larger painting to one side, balancing it with a trio of small prints. Work a three-dimensional item, such as this topiary, into the grouping.

A skirted table offers a generous surface on which to layer a few of your favorite things. For interest, mix short and tall objects, overlapping their edges for a cohesive composition.

s you dream of character-adding accents to carry out your Past Perfect vision, remember that those special touches can take many forms, from collectible objects to decorative projects. Consider the one-of-a-kind charm created by an upholstered bench used as a coffee table. Layers of objects or colors romance a room, too. Drape a scarf of lace or fabric over a mantel, and arrange always-mixable floral and striped pillows on sofas, settees, and window seats. Sponged or ragged, a subtle tone-on-tone painted finish also antiques new walls.

More than a cozy room divider, a floor screen helps you to give your room the right vintage ambience. Simple louvered panels suggest a rural farmhouse. A metal outdoor screen can bring a garden atmosphere inside. A padded and upholstered screen, *left*, adds rich color, its arched panels suggesting the Gothic romance of the 1800s.

An armchair with an aged finish, *left*, assumes even more antiquity when faded florals are added. The back and seat pads simply tie on. In just a few minutes, one easily stenciled motif, *right*, gives collectible cachet to plain closet or cupboard doors. The method? Dab on paint with an almost-dry brush; thin spots add "antiquity." (For instructions on cutting your own stencil, see page 227.)

ometimes white walls simply won't do. That's especially true if your eye loves color and pattern—or if your home lacks the antique ambience that your Past Perfect personality craves. The solution? Rim the room with a wainscot of paneling or a simple chair rail to break up plain-Jane walls and add architectural character. Love the feeling? Take charm a step further by installing charming new glass-paned French doors between the

Blooming wallcoverings and fabrics create cheery getaways that recall the colorful country gardens of the past.

living and dining room or between the dining room and an adjacent hallway. Now, bring on the colorful wallcoverings and fabrics. Here, red and pink flowers warm the dining room walls, while a companion striped fabric romances the chairs. Layered over striped shades, matching floral curtains pull the dining and living rooms together. To keep the flowers from overpowering the spaces, a simple stripe covers the living room walls. The sofa wears a large-scale floral. Inspired by the fabrics, a red-painted coffee tabletop and a bright antique quilt carry out the fresh mood.

With shades of cream and touches of wood for visual relief, a palette of three companion fabrics turns this living-dining area into a "garden" getaway. How to work with several patterns? Remember the no-fail rule: Mix three scales—small, medium, and large. Here, small- and large-scale florals mix easily with midsize stripes.

By blending a bit of formality and informality, you can create a vintage-style living room that hosts formal parties and family gatherings with equal ease.

Fabrics in beiges and taupes mix with taupe paint on the walls and white woodwork for a vintage-style living room that's clean yet serene. A mix of formal and informal decorating touches suits this room, which is used for a variety of occasions. Above the fireplace, *left*, identical groupings of objects flank the centered painting to create formal symmetry. In contrast, an off-center furniture grouping, anchored by an ottoman-turned-coffee table, offers a relaxed welcome. Curtains hung casually by fabric loops and furniture with peeling paint also relax the setting.

Dressing down

Whether casual country or romantic Victorian, all Past Perfect dining rooms share a lack of formality that relaxes family and guests. Time-honored furniture, softened with fabric, creates the comfortable look.

Framed in barn boards, a schoolhouse painting gives this dining spot a view of the past. The plaid wallcovering echoes the no-nonsense look of the farm table, while floral cushions add a hint of romance to ladder-back chairs.

even if you can't slow the pace of life beyond your front door, you can put your dining room in the slow lane when you add friendly furnishings and fabrics. Consider hanging an aged oil painting or two, an old-fashioned print, or framed sepia-toned photographs to establish the faded, vintage mood. Then look for ways to soften the dining pieces themselves. How about sinking into a softly cushioned dining chair, or drawing up to a table that's beautifully skirted to the floor?

Relax the room with soft lighting, too. Put chandeliers on dimmers so you can dial down the brightness, and add charming fabric shades to diffuse the light from once-exposed candelabra bulbs. Whether fine or flea market, mismatched china plates break up formality when you put them to use on the tabletop or arrange them in wall groupings. Pillows and cushions

also can transport even casual dining rooms back in time when their sewn-in details reflect the careful craftsmanship often associated with decades past.

lain pillows? Never. In Past Perfect rooms, piles of pillows clad in a mix of homey prints and trims lend a friendly, gathered-over-time look. For your own mix, vary the shapes and sizes of pillows, then add various edgings, from fabric ruffles to gimp, brush fringe, and ball fringe. Here, even basic boxed cushions have gathered gussets for extra finesse.

When the romance of the past is your decorating destination, let fabric and pattern take you there by softening the hard edges of wooden dining pieces. Charming in its own right, the window seat in this small breakfast room gains more vintage style when a variety of patterned pillows are tossed upon it. The seat serves for solo lounging or extra around-the-table seating. Above it, a simple Roman shade controls light and privacy. For your own vintage scheme, mix patterns, from large florals to small checks and stripes, and vary the shapes and sizes of toss pillows. Because spills are inevitable, consider spraying a stain-resistant treatment on chair cushions and table coverings.

A formal dining room relaxes when easygoing fabrics cover the chairs and windows. Here, cotton slipcovers put the room at ease in two ways: Not only does miniprint fabric itself suggest the breezy feel of summer sundresses, but the fabric also breaks up the potentially staid look often created by matching wood tables and chairs. At the windows, simple curtains are topped by casually gathered (versus fussy pleated or swagged) valances.

Start with your bed

Anyone who longs for the comforts of the past dreams of snuggling into a bed of flowers, especially when it's piled with oodles of pillows and a plump comforter. Put the bed first as you plan your own Past Perfect sleeping spot.

Smaller spaces are ideal when vintage coziness is the goal. Snuggled against the wall and piled with pillows, this bed sets the cottage mood—and doubles for lounging as well as sleeping.

ain or shine, a bedroom keeps spirits bright when it delights the eye with sunny flowers and welcomes the body with soft bedding. Take a look at this example. Inviting, isn't it? It doesn't take much space—or any built-in architectural character—to pull off this kind of decorating magic. Here's the plan: Paint the walls a creamy color. (For a farmhouse feeling, panel the walls first, then paint the paneling.) Next, choose a dominant fabric, such as a fresh floral, for the comforter and curtains. Now layer on the patterns. Here, the comforter turns back to reveal a smaller floral, and the bed skirt itself offers two patterns gathered into charming flounces. A flea market chair adds its own long-ago charm, thanks to a slipcover that includes three different fabrics and a gathered skirt. In small rooms, hang shelves on the wall to display accessories and add character without consuming floor space.

Starting your decorating plans with the bed also means taking a good look at the design of your present headboard and footboard. Is *your* Past Perfect personality confined to the wrong bed? If

To turn back the clock in your bedroom, team a nostalgic bed of wood or metal with a comforter, bed skirt, and array of pillows.

you're dreaming of country inns or grandma's house, your sleep spot is no place for a headboard that's modern—or simply nondescript. Instead, treat yourself to an unabashedly nostalgic design. How about a scrolly metal bed, perhaps in brass or white? A down-home pine or painted sleigh bed? A Shaker four-poster? Shop and measure carefully when considering antique beds; they don't always fit modern-day mattresses and box springs. Happily, reproductions inspired by the romance of the past abound today.

s you plan, create a collected-over-time look by avoiding matching furniture. Break up a roomful of wood with a skirted table and a painted piece or two. Make room to show off your worn treasures, too. Here, new wood moldings create character—and display ledges for plates and art. The fireplace is a fabulous fake—a new surround and mantel, its "firebox" painted black and filled with flowers.

Use solid colors for visual relief and to showcase patterns. For cozy comfort, mix pillow fabrics, trims, and sizes, working from large squares at the back to small breakfast pillows in front. The ruffly valances only look complicated; each has two pockets that are gathered onto two rods.

our spare room can earn its keep as an everyday retreat when you reach confidently beyond your usual decorating limits to immerse yourself in the style of the past. There's nothing timid about the getaway shown here, which takes its inspiration from Scandinavian traditions. The fabrics themselves inspired the scheme, which began with a twin bed that doubles for lounging. Although this unique bed includes fabric insets at each end, a new sleigh bed with matching head- and footboards and an aged finish also would work beautifully. A dowel, hung from the wall or from the ceiling, can support a canopy that simply drapes over the head- and footboards.

Turn a guest room into your own rainy-day getaway with lush fabrics, piles of pillows, and lavish swags and canopies.

For a touch of old-world grandeur, crown a bedroom with a canopy. This version features scalloped edges that repeat on the bed cover. (For canopy instructions, turn to page 227.) A tall tea table and a crystal chandelier suggest Scandinavian rooms of the past. For comfort in a small space, add a lightly scaled, open-arm chair and a cozy ottoman that can slide under a table when not in use.

Anything but spare, the most inviting Past Perfect bedrooms often include an extra furniture piece—or two—for homey comfort. After all, the goal is coziness.

Yes, you can escape to the past—every night—when you take your inspiration from rooms of an earlier era. To begin, climb into your bed and look around. Is the rest of the room ho-hum, or does each element delight your eye by conveying the style and mood you crave? In Past Perfect rooms, you can get away with even more furnishings than usual. Tuck a desk into an attic niche and slide a settee beneath a window, or place it against the foot of the bed. In even the smallest room, you can find a snippet of corner space for an inviting chair and a trim lamp. For more intimacy, consider wallpapering the ceiling or adding a border to lower the room's focus.

Change of attitude

When there's nothing wrong with a room, except that it no longer suits your taste, a fun makeover awaits. Instead of having to solve serious design problems, you can relax and follow your heart to a new scheme.

this bedroom has to keep pace with a young girl whose tastes are growing more sophisticated. Because the parents originally chose classic furniture pieces that would "grow up" with their child, they could splurge on new fabrics and on beautiful, custom-sewn details instead of spending money on a roomful of new furnishings. Whether you're redoing a room for yourself or a child, start by assessing how the room functions. Does the room arrangement still work? Is the bed comfortable? Is there enough storage? Is there some necessary function that the room isn't fulfilling? Next, decide whether the impulse to make a change is prompted by a desire for a different color scheme, a fresh style, or both. To nail down the final vision, take the magazine clipping test, amassing a dozen or more clippings of rooms you or your child love. Analyze what they have in common before you proceed. As you'll see when you turn the page, a love of vintage style—and of pinks and reds— remained, but the goal was to create a warmer, less childlike scheme.

Pattern mixing is easy when you remember to accent a large floral with a geometric stripe. Although a large scale print like this can be overpowering on walls, it's just right for a chair, a comforter, or draperies.

AFTER

BEFORE

Fresh patterns and elegantly sewn details turn a little girl's room into a more sophisticated space that's fit for a teen.

The goal was to brighten the room while also giving it a more traditional look. The method? Retain most of the original furnishings, and use new fabrics and wallcoverings to create a sophisticated scheme that's perfect for a teenage girl—and guests later on. For your own decorating redo, start with the walls. This fresh wallcovering scatters tiny rosebuds around the room, giving the once-dark space a brighter, more spacious look. Against the cheery backdrop, rose prints and stripes gather into feminine rosettes, swags, and jabots. The result? An anything but childlike look enhanced by accessories that imbue the once-country setting with traditional grace. An upholstered armchair, for instance, takes the place of the wicker rocking chair. Similarly, framed wall-hung prints replace the original country accessories. Although the room's metal daybed remains, curtains spilling from a crown of swags and jabots give the sleeping spot newfound intimacy while also balancing the height of the windows.

81

Accent your style

Scout flea markets and antiques stores for furniture to create your Past Perfect style, then layer on accessories new and old.

1 Pair a bamboo bench with a floral rug and wicker baskets to evoke an old-fashioned sunporch.

2 For the more formal side of Past Perfect style, look for creamy ceramic or silver teapots and serving pieces with simple, graceful lines.

3 Look for old side chairs with personality at flea markets and antiques shops. If the chairs are too fragile to sit on, you can use them as sculpture or display space. Small chairs make good side tables to hold books, antique needlepoint pillows, and old dolls.

4 New painted furniture recalls the charm of 19th-century country pieces. Look for pillows with nature motifs—dragonflies are a popular alternative to bees and butterflies.

5 Choose lamps with simple, classic shapes like this modified ginger-jar lamp. Lean prints or paintings against the wall instead of hanging them to suggest a casual mood.

6 "Repurpose" a wicker cart on wheels to hold towels in the bathroom. Create your own cottage-style pedestal table by painting an unfinished table (or a flea market find) and then sanding off paint along the edges that would normally receive wear and tear.

7 Mix crockery, porcelain, and ceramics to create mantel displays. A crock that combines glazed and unglazed decoration has a country-French look; white plates with a raised design recall vintage dessert plates.

8 Bring Scandinavian-inspired country style to your bedroom with a daintily painted bedside chest of drawers. Top a classic urn-shaped lamp with a shade in a muted fabric and layer the bed with pillows for old-fashioned comfort.

9 Assemble accessories with natural textures and simple, unfussy shapes, like these leaf-covered balls and the glazed bowl.

y day, windows fill your home with light and frame your view of the world, but by night, they're black holes. Even if privacy isn't an issue, you'll want to dress your windows to create a snug sense of enclosure in the evening and to filter strong light during the day. In small rooms where draperies would be too fussy or where yards of fabric would overwhelm the space, shades offer a practical and stylish solution. They're easy to make using commercially available patterns. When you choose a lining fabric, think about how the shades will look from outside. A solid ivory fabric is a safe choice, but a subtle pattern in a color that blends with your home's exterior also can be effective.

Buttoned Down

If you don't need to change the position of the shade often, this buttoned-down treatment is a good choice. It's easy to make and there's no hardware involved other than the rod or wood strip you use to install it. You roll the shade toward you, so line the back with a contrasting fabric for interest.

Window Art

With Roman shades, you can showcase an interesting fabric as if it were artwork. These shades are also practical. To block the most light and to provide the best insulation, mount the shade on or just outside the window frame so it covers the opening. A valance hides the hanging mechanism.

If windows are your home's eyes, give them

Tailored and Tidy

Snugly fitted inside the window frame, Roman shades are tailored and neat, pleating into flat folds when raised. Choose this installation to focus attention on attractive woodwork. If you don't want to sew your own shades, purchase them through a catalog and personalize them with a coordinating fabric valance.

Romantic Mystique

For a softer, more romantic look, try a modified Roman shade with tails. Mounted outside the window frame, it provides good light control and insulation. Even when raised, however, this style of shade hides a lot of the window, so use it where privacy is important or views are not.

something fashionable to wear: fabric shades.

windows

town&country inspirations

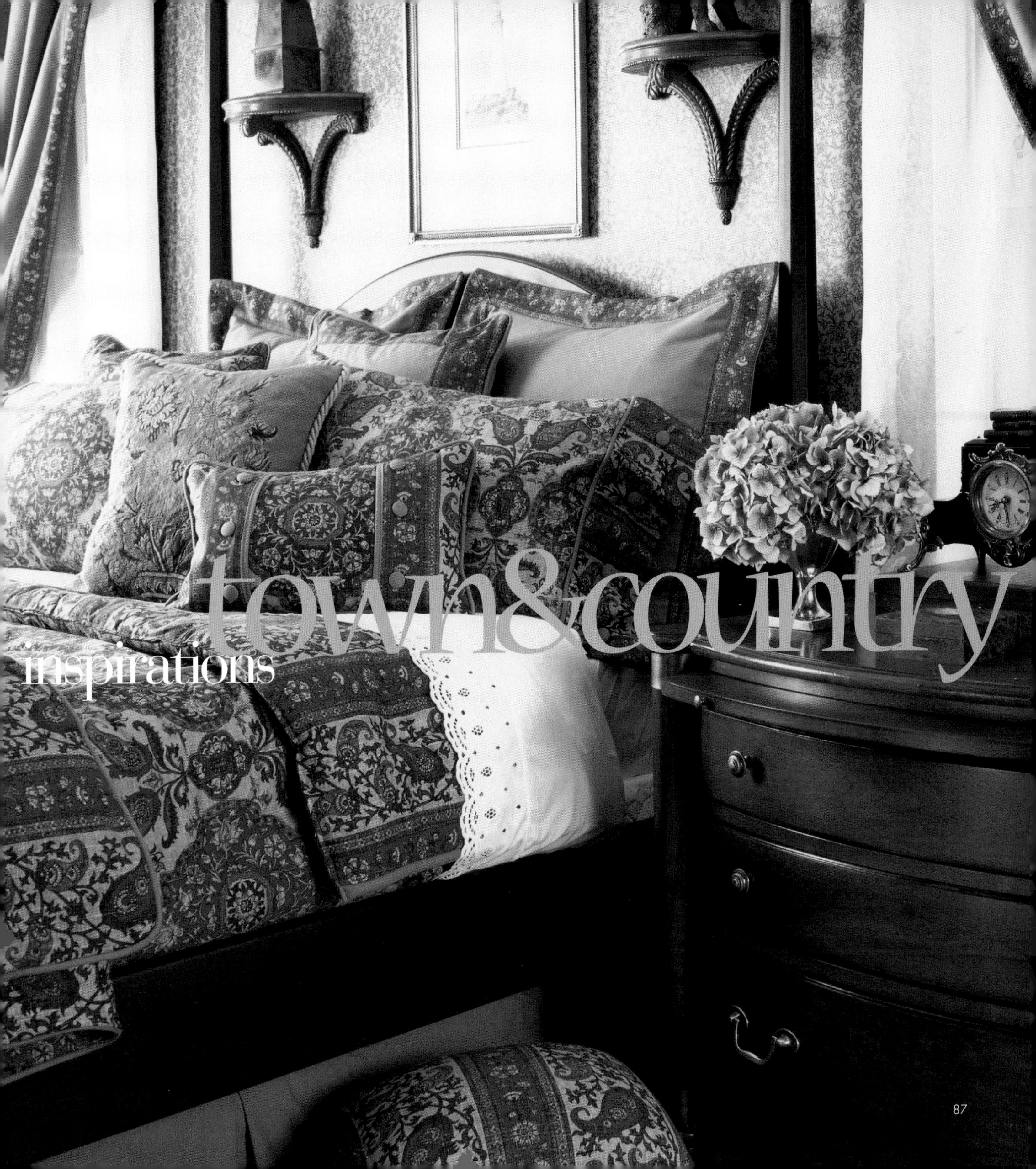

timeless, tailored, classic, daring. The hallmark of this style is an intimate, clubbish elegance that lends itself to both casual and formal settings. The tools for creating it include strong colors, bold shapes, and decorative accents drawn from the arts of many cultures. Fabrics feature motifs based on architectural elements, Oriental carpets, Flemish tapestries, or paisley shawls. When florals appear, they're splashed on surprisingly dark backgrounds for an effect that's decorative but not dainty. Classical accessories—urns, columns, architectural fragments—mix easily with ethnic art and handcrafted objects in Town and Country rooms. Furnishings range from English Regency and Biedermeier antiques to bamboo, contemporary iron, and glass. The resulting mix suggests a sophisticated world traveler who assembles fabrics and accessories with a confident, educated eye and a strong sense of individual taste.

Tailored by design

With its classic roots and global references, the Town and Country style taps into your dreams of being a globe-trotting adventurer. It's essentially a bold, no-fuss approach to comfort and design.

he owners of this 1920s Craftsman-style bungalow have a strong appreciation for family history. When they began looking for a house, they wanted a place that would reflect that appreciation and provide a suitable setting for creating traditions of their own. The inherent character and architectural details of this cottage offered the perfect starting point. With the help of interior designer Austin Rese, the couple decorated and furnished it in a comfortable, tailored style that accommodates relaxation, entertaining, and family life for a busy, two-career couple with a young child.

Because the living room and dining room connect visually and physically, the design required a color and fabric palette that would link the two yet give each its own character. Accordingly, the walls in both spaces were painted with a flat, off-white paint, then stenciled with a leaf design in off-white semigloss paint. The treatment gives subtle texture to

To make a stairwell feel and function as part of the living area, take a tip from these homeowners: turn the space into an art gallery. Here, identically matted and framed pressed botanical specimens fill the area. They're hung in a regular grid for an orderly look.

the walls. Fabrics in both rooms reflect the couple's no-fuss, sophisticated tastes, with an emphasis on neutrals, olive green, and gold. A leaf-print fabric that includes the main colors appears in both rooms, covering a chair and pillows in the living room and swagging the draperies in the dining room.

To open up the square living room visually, the designer angled the sofa across one corner (see *page 90*). With a fabric-covered folding screen behind the sofa, this area becomes a focal point balancing a massive stone fireplace (not shown). A generously proportioned ottoman doubles as a coffee table, and side chairs cozy up to the sofa without blocking the view of the fireplace.

To give walls a whisper of texture and pattern, apply stencils or stripes in semigloss over a flat base of the same color.

family heirlooms and antiques accent new furnishings in the living and dining areas. A chest made by the wife's grandmother serves as an end table; an heirloom clock occupies pride of place on the sideboard in the dining room. The framed, pressed botanical specimens on the stairwell wall and in the dining room are pages from a 19th-century French student's field notes, found in a Paris flea market. The designer had them matted and framed identically to unify them. Treated as artwork, they refer back to the leaf-print fabric and evoke that globe-trotting Town and Country adventurer.

Echoing the sofa decoration, brass furniture tacks outline the simple, bold curves of the upholstered dining chairs. Striped panels at the windows can be exchanged for sheers in the summer. The floral swags stay in place year-round.

Color by degrees

What's your comfort level when it comes to color? Do bold colors overwhelm you? Or do lighter values leave you cold? Here are three ways to dip into color to create the mood you want in your rooms.

One color plus white makes an easy, no-fail starting point for creating a color scheme you can live with. Choose a color you love (revisit the color quiz on pages 16–19 if you need to). Then decide whether you want to use the pure version of that color, a lighter tint, or a darker shade of it. The pure hue plus white can be lively and bold. Go with tints of the hue for a softer, quieter look; choose darker shades for a richer, more formal feeling.

One light-value color plus white, like the rose-red opposite, yields a fresh, airy effect. Combining a dark-value color—navy blue, for example—with white produces a high-contrast mix that's more dramatic in feeling. Browse through fabric samples and wallpaper books to find a one-color-plus-white pattern that appeals to you, then use that as your starting point for assembling coordinating patterns and a solid. Your scheme will be richer if you include accents in a darker

Give depth and weight to a one-color-plus-white scheme with accessories and accents in a darker value of the main color. The red tones of the side table, the books, picture frame, and wooden apples all serve that purpose here.

or purer version of your color. The rose-red pillows in the sunroom at right help ground the lighter hue that's in the stripes, plaids, and florals.

Almost any one-color-plus-white scheme will be more satisfying if you add touches of a color from the opposite side of the color wheel (see *pages 26–27*). In the room at right, plants supply notes of soft green to cool down the overall warmth of the rose-red and rose-pink hues.

If you like stronger color and a slightly more complex color scheme, choose fabrics and wallpapers that combine one color plus white with a complementary accent. In the photo on *page 99*, a scheme of sage green and white gains emphasis when the claret-red from the drapery is pulled out and used on the side chair.

ed is the direct opposite of green on the color wheel, but you're not limited to a literal interpretation of color-wheel dynamics in building your scheme. If your main color is warm (yellows, oranges, reds), your complementary accent can be any of the cool colors (greens, blues, violets). In

Color sets the mood. Check the quiz on page 16 to find out how colors make you feel and which is right for you.

Give definition to furniture shapes with piping. Here, a darker value of red outlines the amply proportioned rolled-arm sofas. Adding a few accent pillows in the same hue helps anchor the simple, light-value color scheme. Green plants add contrast.

the living room on the facing page, navy blue and deep red are nearly equally distributed around the room so that neither dominates. Large amounts of light color keep the overall effect from being too intense.

f you're hungering for still bolder color and more complexity, turn up the heat by increasing the amount of rich, warm color in the mix (see *page 100*). Or choose a pair of complements and add accents of a neigboring color. In the living room on *page 101*, a muted gold and burgundy striped fabric brings together colors from opposite sides of the wheel. Touches of royal blue enliven and brighten the combination.

For a more complex scheme, add a complementary color to one-color-plus-white. The complement may be an accent, like the chair *above*, or the two colors may be equally weighted, as in the room *opposite*. The mix of red, white, and blue feels perfectly balanced because no one color dominates. In both rooms, a floral with a white ground provides the key to the color choices and helps link the contrasting colors in the overall room scheme.

Add luxury to simple pinch-pleat draperies
with an "overskirt" trimmed in long fringe.
Use a shorter fringe on the leading edges.

To create a rich, formal look, *page 101*, choose fabrics in darker shades and sofas and chairs that have strong shapes. To express a Town and Country personality, look for tapestries or fabrics with heraldic motifs, Empire-style furnishings, and accessories with classic lines. For a cozier, clubbier version of the style, *left*, use purer color—warm red instead of burgundy—and choose orderly florals or stripes on a white ground to balance the warm tones of fabric and wood.

Go boldly

There's nothing timid about a Town and Country dining room. A gathering place where conversation flows by the glow of candlelight, it asserts its sophisticated style through scale, pattern, and color.

the key to this decorating style is boldness, whether it's in the proportions of the furniture, the assertiveness of the pattern, or the strength of the color. If you love strong color *and* classic pattern, start with a wallpaper or a combination of wallpapers and borders to create architectural character in a ho-hum space. Install a chair rail as in the room shown on *page 102*, to physically separate the dado from the upper wall. A malachite-patterned paper on the dado is rich and formal, and the solid color anchors the stripes above. Installing the swagged wallpaper border so it turns each corner properly calls for some planning. You'll need to start in one corner and then as you approach the next corner, stop and work from that corner back, piecing the motif where the two strips meet.

If you don't yet own a dining table, decide first what shape table your space can accommodate. In a square

Consider contrasting elegant, weighty furniture and classical wallpaper with simple sheer curtains hung from decorative knobs. The contrast of the gutsy and the gossamer introduces a breezy freshness to the room.

Include a touch of black in the room, the traditional rectangular banquet table probably won't room for elegance. Candles, metal lamps, or picture mats can supply the right accent. fit, but a round pedestal table or a square one will be perfect. Furniture with overscaled proportions, like the pedestal table and console on *page 102*, will give your room Town and Country personality, but so will the warm wood and deeply carved moldings of a country French sideboard or antique cabinet. If your table doesn't have the mass to balance such furnishings, add visual heft with a floor-length table skirt in a bold pattern.

Color can create the mood as well. Warm red walls stimulate appetites and conversation; deep purple, midnight blue, and dark green are also dramatic choices for the dining room. By the glow of candlelight, these colors will make the room feel intimate and exciting. To keep the dark colors from feeling oppressive, paint windows and woodwork white.

If you prefer lighter colors, let your daring personality emerge with table coverings and slipcovers that can be whisked away after the dinner is over. Damask-patterned velvets, tapestries, and florals with black backgrounds make rich, dramatic cloths and runners. Upholstering Parsons-style dining chairs in these fabrics turns your dining room into a

Give plain draperies a weightier presence by hanging them on oversize rods and curtain rings just below the crown molding. Add fringe and tassels for elegance. In a room with light walls and dark wood furniture, use fabric as the visual bridge between the light and dark tones.

salon where guests will want to linger. To impart this feeling to other styles of dining chairs, cover the seats with fabric that matches the tablecloth and make tabard-style slipcovers to tie over the chair backs.

The one item you *don't* want to be bold or overscaled is the centerpiece. If guests are seated around the table, the centerpiece should be low enough for guests to talk to each other without having to peer around flower stems. It's also thoughtful to keep candle flames above or below eye level.

Red stimulates conversation and appetites, so it's a good choice for dining room walls. White trim adds crispness.

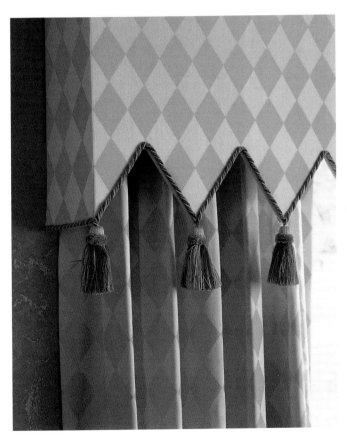

Inspired by the fabric pattern, the cornices *left* and *page 106* are shaped into diamond points following the fabric motif. To echo the diamond shape and bring the colors of the walls and draperies together, the chair seats were stitched from triangles of contrasting fabrics.

Defining drama

Can a bedroom be both dramatic and comfortable? In a sense, it depends on how you define drama—and comfort. Commanding furnishings and courageous colors can create a feeling of rock-solid security.

Warm up a black-and-white scheme with wood or brass accents. Nested tables, usually found in a living room, are perfect for a guest room, where the lower table can hold a guest's belongings.

Color contrast is a well-accepted way to create drama in decorating. High-contrast color schemes excite the eye and create a sense of energy—not necessarily the feeling you want to evoke in a bedroom. If you find the stark severity of black and white restful and clean, however, this high-contrast combination may offer just what you need to relax.

Large blocks of strong color also can create a welcoming cocoon that's both dramatic and comfortable (see *pages 112–13*). This usually works best if the colors lean toward intense but muted tones (as if some black had been added) rather than pure, clear color. An olive or forest green, for example, is bold but quieter than a kelly green.

If you don't like waking up to lots of color, let your furnishings create the drama. A distinctive bed with a massive headboard or character-filled shape will define the room's

personality. If your bed is ordinary, give it presence with a wall-mounted valance and curtains, or with a canopy hung from the ceiling or the wall above the bed (see *pages 75* and *81* for treatments that could work for Town and Country style if executed in different fabrics).

emphasize the notion of comfort with piles of pillows, combining oversize cushions with rectangular and square ones and with long bolsters or neck rolls. Such extravagance isn't just for looks—if you enjoy reading in bed, those stacks of pillows will support your back

If your guest room needs to double as a home office, bring in a daybed and stack it with pillows so it looks like a sofa.

Turn a basic twin bed into a daybed by raising the mattress on a frame of 2x4s (see page 228 for directions). Have fun with accessories—layer a faux zebra skin rug over the carpet and combine pillows with different patterns, trims, and textures.

and neck. On a daybed or banquette, bolsters stand in for armrests. Toss on a plump comforter or duvet (a plain, down-filled comforter with a decorative, removable cover) to make the bed look and *feel* inviting.

even if your walls are plain and your furniture unexciting, you can create drama with the fabric you choose for the spread, comforter, and pillows. An elegant, large-scale pattern based on a classic motif, such as paisley or Turkish-carpet medallions, will bring Town and Country style to the bedroom. Florals with a dark ground

Let tailored treatments create a mood of serenity in the bedroom. Keep clutter to a minimum, too, but pamper yourself with touchable textures.

also can work. Or, if you prefer a minimum of pattern in the bedroom, choose colors you love in rich, sensuous textures of velvet, chenille, damask, and fine wool.

Take the drama to the windows, too, with heavy velvet or wool draperies or treatments with deep valances and luxurious bullion fringe.

Paint the walls a warm, dark hue as a background for sumptuous fabrics in spice tones. Leaving the iron bed uncanopied emphasizes its strong lines and underscores the graphic effect of large blocks of color.

To link the bedroom and bath in a master suite, use similar wallpapers and at least one of the same fabrics in each room. Here, to keep the bathroom as light-filled as possible, the airy print that covers the bed also dresses the bathroom windows. A small-scale striped wallpaper in the bath coordinates with the larger stripe in the bedroom. If you like to read in bed, consider upholstering the headboard in a soft-textured material. To give the bed added grandeur, install a cornice with sheers and draperies just below the ceiling to frame the headboard.

To let your signature print in the bedroom speak most clearly, use it in at least three high-impact areas, such as the windows, the bed skirt or spread, and the bed cornice and curtains.

Make your statement with the bed or with fabric. The massive proportions of the antique sleigh bed, *left,* won't fit every bedroom, but even scaled-down versions will create a Town and Country look. If you have high ceilings, create a snug feeling by draping a fabric panel over a pair of curtain rods suspended from the ceiling. You can find Empire-style beds, *center,* at antiques shops and estate sales. A reversible duvet lets you change the look of the room for the seasons, with a light-color fabric for summer and a dark-ground floral for winter. If your bed is more modestly proportioned, *right,* let the fabric do the work. Choose a large-scale pattern that's more architectural than floral and use it on the comforter, pillow shams, and draperies. Tailored pillow shams, bed skirt, and window treatments emphasize the unfussy character of the Town and Country style.

Revive a tired comforter by stitching up a duvet
cover from flat sheets or cotton upholstery fabric.
Use covered buttons to fasten the duvet in place.

Total transformation

Tastes change, and the light, sweet look you once loved suddenly no longer satisfies. Here's a dramatic example of how fabric—and creative vision—can give your bedroom a whole new personality.

Originally, this suburban bedroom featured Shaker-style furniture combined with a romantic floral for a 1980s country look (see *page 121*). It wasn't much to the husband's taste, and the wife was open to change, so they consulted interior designer Darlene Siwik, who had helped them with other projects.

To turn the bedroom into a master suite, the designer enclosed the bed with curtains and used end-of-bed space for a pair of armchairs and a table. Fabric upholsters the walls for a rich, textured look.

Her first suggestion was to rearrange the floor plan. The bedroom is long and narrow with a sloping dormer wall above the windows. Moving the bed into the corner and placing it on the diagonal helped square up the room visually. It also created space at the end of the bed for a pair of armchairs and a small table. Angling the bed also played down the sloping section along the window wall.

Next, she proposed cozying up the room by upholstering the walls with fabric and giving the bed a sense of enclosure with a canopy and curtains. The posts on the couple's bed weren't tall enough for a drapery treatment to hang properly, however, so the designer had a carpenter add 12-inch sections with finials. The

AFTER

The bedroom, *below*, gets a glamour makeover, *left*, with a fearless mix of fabrics. Clockwise from *top left, page 120*: If you find a wonderful trim or fringe but can only afford a little of it, use it to trim an accent pillow. Layer pillows of different sizes and shapes for richness. To determine whether a fabric will work well for tied-back draperies, gather it up in one hand to see how easily it forms soft folds. For a rich effect, combine non-working draperies with privacy shades. A painted chest of drawers with a crackle finish provides both storage and bedside service. Flat ties stitched to the borders of the bed curtains attach the reversible panels to the bed frame. Ties also hold the reversible canopy in place, stretched taut over the top of the frame.

Don't worry about matching colors exactly. The eye will blend subtle differences and see the room as a finished product.

carpenter also added the frame around the top and finished the wood so it harmonized with the original light pine.

The palette of fabrics started with the floral for the bed curtains. Ultimately, it included 14 different textiles, with a blend of textures and patterns of varying scales. The result is an "evolved" look that's rich, inviting, and a little exotic.

BEFORE

Accent your style

If you're a Town and Country personality, you have a wide variety of accessories from which to choose to help you create the look.

1 Shop for accessories that suggest global influences. A creamy ceramic Moroccan vase encased in brass fretwork evokes the Near East, and an iron bell suggests Asian temple bells. Showcase family photos in bone and faux-tortoiseshell picture frames.

2 Present fragments of ethnic textiles as art—look for bold, graphic patterns. Weathered benches can work in this style if paired with striped silk pillows and cushions.

3 Assemble objects with classical references, such as museum reproductions and urn-shaped lamp bases or vases. Choose decorative items with natural textures such as horn, wood, and leather for robust but elegant accents.

4 Antiques with an attitude and old prints of European sites recall the Grand Tour, a required travel experience for cultured gentlemen of the 18th century. An antique clock makes a perfect focal point for a display, even if it no longer keeps time.

5 English hunt themes suggest the "Country" side of Town and Country. Scout flea markets or antiques shops for miniature reproductions, watercolors, or postcards to frame and hang below a mantel or above a doorway.

6 Trophy cups, whether turned into lamp bases or used as vases, conjure up the sporting life. Purchase a silver tray table like this one or create your own by resting a silver tray on top of an old folding luggage rack or a custom-made stand.

7 Combine classic shapes, from obelisks to urns to Queen-Anne furnishings.

8 Set the table in Town and Country style with collectible china featuring hunt motifs.

9 Put something quirky underfoot, such as a rug resembling leopard spots. The bull's-eye mirror offers timeless design and traditional elegance.

rrrrr...Do icy-white walls leave your rooms feeling cold? Banish the big chill with a warm wrap of wallcoverings. Depending on your taste, consider the serious or the whimsical, one allover pattern or an eye-catching mix of wallcoverings and companion borders. The goal is to give your rooms the friendly character that you and your personality crave. The method? Start by finding a color cue: Are there adjoining rooms and palettes to consider, or is yours a stand-alone space? Do you want the room to refresh you with bright, sunny ambience or relax you with a muted palette? These four looks—understated, witty, mellow, and romantic—show you how to turn up the heat on any chilly space.

Borders with Character

Patterns that suggest sponging give plain walls fresh dimension and a look of age, *left*. To break up flat expanses, install a chair rail one-third of the way up the wall; hang striped paper below it and solid above. The finale? A double border for architectural oomph and color contrast.

Witty Trompe l'Oeil

A just-for-fun collection of books may not enrich your mind, but it will delight your eye and give a dull den bookish character and witty charm. Here, the wallcovering not only sets the mood but also establishes a classic blue-and-red color scheme that's carried out by curtains and upholstery.

Why shiver in a room of arctic-white walls?

Inviting Entry

Use a large-scale pattern to cozy up an oversize space like this entry hall. To avoid cluttering an area that's broken up by doorways and windows, forget busy borders and chair rails and choose one richly colored wall covering for warmth without fussiness.

Romantic Bedroom

Wallcoverings in pastel yellow warm a bedroom in more ways than one. The color imbues the space with a toasty feeling, while borders create intimacy by rescaling the space. One border visually lowers the ceiling; the other offers a snug embrace at headboard level.

walls

It's so easy to add warm ambience with colorfully patterned walls.

inspirations modern living

fresh, lighthearted, lively, eclectic, crisp. This clean, dynamic style expresses fresh energy, light-hearted spirit, and design confidence. The furnishings may be a mix of traditional, modern, and flea market, but the glorious results are anything but faded. Upholstered pieces, new or old, wear snappy prints, plaids, stripes, or checks. Even floral fabrics feature lots of white space around the motifs for an airy look that adds punch to colors while giving graphic patterns room to breathe. Walls are as likely to be decorated with a weathered piece of barn board as with whimsical original art. Other accessories, such as lamps and vases, may feature simple sculptural shapes and bright, clear colors. But there's plenty of room for vintage collectibles and pieces of furniture that look as if they've come from grandma's attic. When contrasted with fresh, clean color and patterns, these aged objects not only add a feeling of stability, but also offer a dose of sassy personality.

Fresh and fun

One look at the mini "meadow" growing on this coffee table, and visitors know they're in for some decorating fun. In fact, this coffee-table tableau says a lot about this owner's Modern Living style.

n tune with this home's quaint 1940s exterior, the interior spaces blend familiar, friendly seating pieces with fresh colors and modern accessories for a look that's cottage, contemporary—and oh-so-chic. The starting point for this scheme? The fabric store where the owner shopped with two things in mind: her favorite color—blue—and a desire to reenergize her once-dark rooms. A new seersucker plaid, teamed with solid blue and solid yellow fabrics, fit the bill, inspiring a sunny new scheme guaranteed to lift the spirits.

Before you turn the page and see the living room, take a close look at the coffee table. A checked cloth adds a homey touch and reinforces a tangy color scheme that's carried out with shapely new glass vases. Sown in a neat row in a metal planter, waving wheat grass delights the eye and guarantees a smile.

Forget your toes—you can wiggle your *nose* in blades of grass when they're planted on the coffee table. Decidedly casual (and definitely fun), the gathering of grass sets a friendly mood for a happy mix of books and sculptural vases set atop a colorful checked cloth.

To plan your own eye-popping palette, remember that in modern rooms opposites *do* attract. Once you've chosen a dominant fabric pattern—one that you can't live without—answer this question, "How bold can you go?" Here, the blue-and-white seersucker makes a snappy starting point, but it's the the contrast between hot yellow, cool blue, and airy white that gives the room its confidence and

Does your room suffer from the blahs? To reinvigorate the same old space, go for a happy, high-contrast color scheme.

energy. This great scheme could have ended with the new slipcovers, but the owner took one more brave step, rolling yellow on the walls for a spirited glow.

se some decorative sleight of hand to enliven rooms with fresh surprises, too. Here, curtains mounted on wide rods installed on the wall above the windows add height and width to the same old panes. The white fabric not only provides visual relief, but also brightens the room by amplifying every ray of precious sunlight. In addition, the yellow walls themselves add an illusion of daylong sunshine to this space, which receives little of the real thing through its north- and east-facing windows.

Mixed greens provide finishing touches. Plants and flowers (tucked—surprise!—into wall-hung vases) keep the bright yellow in check, as does the understated grass-green rug.

A lively palette, casual prints, and natural touches set a friendly mood. The brushed-metal accents and snappy yellow cording help give the cottage-style room its modern edge. For ottoman slipcover instructions, see page 228.

The confident contrast that gives Modern Living schemes their liveliness takes many forms, from the interplay of opposing colors to the pairing of disparate materials and textures. Linked by a blue-and-yellow palette and a casual mood, bright

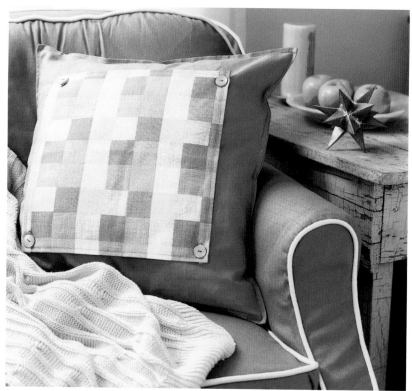

fabrics live with peeling-paint tables, and mellow wood dining pieces coexist with modern metal accents. The living room's yellow walls frame a view into the dining spot, where calming blue paint and golden woods slow the pace for meals. In such small spaces, just a dash of appetizing fruit-patterned fabric can set the mood and color scheme.

Wooden brackets screwed into studs that frame the sliding glass door, *below*, support a shelf that displays a bold and beautiful lineup of pitchers, pots, and plates. Just for fun, the valance's scalloped hem follows the lines of the fabric's banana motif. For shelf and valance how-to, see pages 229–30.

Anything but buttoned-up, this outgoing chair, *above*, gets sassy style from bright piping and a toss pillow accented with a buttoned-on "bib." A lime-green throw adds juicy color, while an aged table proudly wears a coat of peeling paint.

Pattern plays

Modern Living personalities prefer rooms that live on the edge, graphically speaking. Love the dynamic energy of checks, plaids, or stripes? Here's how to build your own scheme around a crisp geometric.

So you've fallen in love with one colorful, geometric pattern. What next? Here, bold plaid caught the owner's eye, but it's the mix of novelty print curtains and a smaller plaid on the chair that knits the plaid sofa into the room. The basic pattern-mixing guideline—mix three scales for harmony—plays out beautifully here. The large, bright plaid doesn't overpower the space, because it's balanced by the combined visual weight of the small plaid on the armchair and midsize motif on the curtains. Solid colors on pillows and walls provide visual relief from the pattern, as does a neutral sisal rug.

When working with straight-line geometric prints, introduce a few sinuous accessories or patterns for flowing contrast. Here, a rounded end table, an urn-base lamp, and the decorative apron on the coffee table offer curvy counterpoint to the fabrics' hard-edged patterns.

Shared colors turn a variety of prints into a happy family of patterns. The palette of green and white shown here comes alive when sunny yellow and complementary reds enter the picture. Lots of white keeps the dynamic scheme in check.

In contrast to the previous living room, the inviting gathering spot here began with a more subtle sofa fabric—a check in analogous blue, purple, and green. Working with a disparate collection of meant-to-be-mixed fabrics, the owner tossed on pillows clad in a bold stripe and a viny floral motif. So far so good, but it was the reupholstering of two armchairs—one with a floral stripe, the other with a bolder cabana stripe— that creates this interesting pattern play.

If you're into eclectic design, use a coordinated group of three or more fabrics to create a look that's pulled together but not too "matched."

beyond the conversation area, the eclectic look flows to the windows, where the treatments, though visually compatible, differ both in style and in pattern. Curtains in a diamond and floral design gather behind the sofa, and striped Roman shades treat the landing windows.

As always, modern spirit manifests itself in the confidence to mix. Checks and stripes join with sculptural vases, sleek lamps, and trim window shades for a crisp look. In contrast, florals, turned legs, aged finishes, and the slightly gathered corners on the otherwise tailored sofa slipcover nod to the past.

A flea market coffee table sets the stage for a delightful blend of the modern and the mellow. Clean-lined geometric fabrics, vases, and lamps play off against hints of the past—a Shaker chair, an aged chest, and a salvaged door hung as "art."

Bright colors, bold checks, and down-home accessories create a living space that satisfies both modern design sensibilities and a yen for the country. Here, soft-green sponged walls provide a mellow background for a vibrant scheme. On the sofa slipcover, charmingly rendered fruit motifs are organized within a grid—a frankly square theme echoed by the bold checkerboard fabric that

Gently gather fabric and drape it over dowels or loop it through rings for a quick, countrified swag, *above left*. For added finesse, cut the trailing edges at an angle and hem before draping. Use scraps of your favorite new fabrics to customize your room's accessories,

above right. Here, fruit motifs affixed with spray adhesive adorn a lampshade. Checked fabric customizes picture mats, too. Cut mat board to fit standard 8x10-inch frames, leaving a 4x6-inch opening for your photo. Wrap mats with fabric and affix with spray adhesive.

skirts the chair pads. A swag consisting of a length of coordinating striped fabric simply draped over two wooden dowels reinforces both the color scheme and the look of back-roads simplicity. Behind the swag, a Roman shade banded with the same stripe as the swag provides a sleek touch as it controls light and offers privacy.

a s with any pattern play, decorative accessories form the essential supporting cast. Here, they carry out the eclectic, country-modern look set by the starring sofa. Checked picture mats, cut from fabric scraps, add punch to the walls. A simple wicker coffee table combines the best of country-porch charm, yet its clean lines and lack of decoration give it a touch of modern style, too. Affixed with spray adhesive, fruit motifs cut from the sofa fabric customize a lampshade.

When softened with new seat pads, cottage-style dining chairs, *right,* create charming, comfy seating in the living room. Checkerboard skirts add the fun. For a collected look, consider staining one chair and treating the other to a crackle-painted finish. Mix fabrics on toss pillows, *page 143,* to create your own style. Here solid red plays up the room's dominant hue, while scraps of striped fabric, sewn into an intriguing design, make a one-of-a-kind pillow.

Simple checks and stripes join juicy fruits in a room that's as fresh and friendly as a farmhouse kitchen. Bold red against white pleases modern eyes.

Dining light

For Modern Living personalities, "dining light" has as much to do with decorating as with diet. Modern or traditional, furniture pieces show off their lines against airy backgrounds, and color schemes evoke a smile.

ontrast is the key ingredient in dining spots that exude the lighthearted appeal and design confidence that typify Modern Living schemes. Consider the visual intrigue created when antique chairs pull up to a modern table, or the eye-popping energy produced when two or three dynamic colors collide on a panel of fabric. As you'll see, even serenely patternfree schemes satisfy modern personalities when light tones play against dark and solid colors stand in opposition to each other.

For starters, feast on the anything-but-timid dining room here, which delights with contrasts at every turn. Cool blues, hot pinks, sunny yellows, and shady greens recall an invigorating walk through field and woods. Varied prints, from plaid to painterly florals, large and small, cover the unmatched chairs—curvaceous traditional designs that flirt charmingly with the clean-lined contemporary dining table.

Linked both by colors that uplift the spirit and a clean design approach that showcases each piece like sculpture, a collection of shapely chairs gathers around a classic Parsons table. The sleek runner echoes the table's lines.

Confidence—to mix different moods as well as styles—not only creates interesting rooms, but it can result in especially functional ones as well. Any dining room can work from dawn until dark, hosting everything from casual family breakfasts to dinners for the boss. The trick? A light wallcovering and simple window treatments that fade into the backdrop, allowing a wardrobe of skirts and slipcovers to alter the look of the room in a flash. Take a look at this example. In the morning, garden florals and easygoing plaid sound a bright wake-up call. For an evening occasion, the table dons a long damask or linen skirt, or lets its gleaming wood show with only a runner for color. The chairs change, too, from casual floral daytime dresses to red damask when it's party time.

A wardrobe of skirts, table-cloths, and slipcovers can help a dining room serve everything from casual breakfast to formal dinner.

ven if your walls and window treatments are more heavily colored and patterned, you still can use solid-color fabrics to take the formal edge off a dining room—and to add personal style by breaking up a potentially staid set of matching wood dining pieces. Leave beautifully designed wood chairs exposed, and toss a skirt over the table, or do the reverse, slipping floor-length dresses on the chairs and baring the wood table.

Friendly floral and plaid fabrics relax a dining room for everyday gatherings. When a formal dinner is in the offing, the table skirts are pulled off to expose the fine wood beneath, and the flowered slipcovers are removed to reveal dressier red damask upholstery.

Crisp yellow-and-white checks provide a geometric background for this charming fabric and wall-covering. The print sets a bright and happy mood that's carried out by a just-for-fun table topper with pennant edges rimmed in snappy stripes. The solid blue table skirt serves as a calming influence in a room filled with bold pattern and bright yellow.

Come on, get happy—and snappy—with energizing yellow checks.

o make a dining room as easy to live with as it is to look at, treat chair and table fabrics with a stain-resistant spray. Be sure to wipe up spills immediately. To keep colors bright and beautifully sewn accessories, such as this table topper, in good shape, it's best to avoid machine-washing even durable cottons. Dry cleaning is gentler to fibers and colors than laundering.

Brave color contrast and a bit of bold geometry create a light and bright feeling that satisfies Modern Living personalities. Anything but serious, a sunny zigzag topper gives the dining table a modern edge.

Visual puns add humor, too. The classic blue-and-white "porcelain" teacups and bowls on the fabric and wallcovering manifest in three-dimensional form on the table and shelves.

For a dining nook with bed-and-breakfast charm, mix feminine touches with dashes of vibrant colors over white, *above*. An iron-base table and a viny floral wallcovering set the stage for a bright yet romantic look that's carried out with printed sheer fabric fashioned into curtains and seat-cushion skirts. In glorious fruit-salad hues, farm-fresh patterns, *center*, stimulate spirits as well as appetites. The design recipe for this room is easy: Blend two coordinating prints on the wall, adding a shelf between the patterns as display space. Fabric-clad chairs pull up to a table accented with bright mats. Stitch up a pointy valance, or toss napkins over a rod for a quick topper. To banish formality, *right*, relax your room with an easygoing fruit-pattern wallcovering often associated with the kitchen. Chairs dressed in casual plaid also issue a friendly invitation.

Working from the walls in, give even a formal dining room the happy colors and visual surprises that your Modern Living personality demands. Bright colors and informal, unexpected novelty prints are just the beginning.

There are no excuses for sleepy eyes or tired spirits when you give your kitchen the same energetic style as the rest of your house. Use Modern Living staples—colorful counterpoint or graphic pattern—to create your own recipe. Ease into the day, *right*, with pastels. Dollops of cream and garnishes of red create the contrast. Or, brew up a caffeinelike jolt for the eyes with bright red-and-white checks and cheery cherry accents on a bold black-and-white floor, *page 153*. A blue, green, and white stripe at the windows offers cooling contrast and picks up the colors of the foliage in the fruit-patterned wallpaper and table skirt fabric.

Good morning! Add zip to a boring line-up of white cabinets—and zest to your kitchen dining experiences—with color-ful wallcoverings and fabrics.

Sleep tight

Your bed is—or should be—a magic carpet that transports you to the restful realm of dreams. To ensure a good trip, pick patterns and colors to please the eye and soft textures and pillowy surfaces to comfort the body.

hink of it this way: You're on the road for about eight hours *every* night, so you may as well travel not only in style, but in comfort, too. Sit in your bed for a minute, look around, *feel* around, and decide: Are you going first class or in coach? Assuming that your mattress and box springs are in good shape, consider the downy extras that can make the difference between sweet dreams and a bumpy ride. First, build a nest of pillows, including down or down-and-feather pillows for softness, and others with firmer foam fillings to lean against for late-night reading or breakfast in bed. Now, lighten your load by dumping a weighty pile of blankets in favor of an almost gossamer down-filled comforter. To protect the comforter, slip it into a ready-made or custom-sewn duvet cover. Love the soft feeling? Go a step further and plop a featherbed on top of your mattress for smooth sailing to dreamland—and back.

Crisp, yet comfortable, this room makes an irresistible time-out spot. A modern rendition of a design classic, the sleigh bed piled with pillows creates a cozy sense of enclosure. Bright florals and plaid rev up the energy level.

Watch out! Shopping for fabric is a little like dating—you may fall head over heels in love at any moment. When a particular pattern grabs your heart, don't fight the feeling. That pattern can inspire an irresistible new look—and an easy-to-create one when you use ready-made linens. First, choose a pattern, then decide how far you want to take it.

end to be fickle? Opt for neutral walls so you can change the look on a whim simply by remaking the bed. Or, if you prefer a long-term relationship with one beloved pattern, then slather it on the walls, too. Either way, plan for subtle changes by creating a variety of mix-and-match pillows and buying blankets in two or three different colors.

Same fabrics, two approaches: Love change? With neutral walls, *page 156*, redecorating a bedroom is as easy as changing the sheets and hanging fresh curtains. In the summer, flowers abound, but rugged plaids can move in when winter comes. Prefer to make a commitment? Add wallcoverings, *right*, to create a perennial, year-round "garden."

To turn your bedroom into a retreat you can't resist, let your heart be your guide: Start with one must-have fabric.

Some like it hot—and some don't. As you shop for pattern, consider how colors can affect your psyche. (In case you missed it, take our color quiz on pages 16–18 to learn more.) Inherently relaxing, cool greens, purples, or blues have a place in most bedroom schemes, but it's up to you to find a balance between cool and warm colors that's right for your eye.

Should you emphasize warm or cool colors? Here's a clue: Do you prefer bright sunrises or clear moonlit nights?

ool colors taken from the fabrics dominate in this bedroom, delighting and refreshing the water-loving homeowner with images of a dip in the lake. Textured and sponged, the blue walls set the watery backdrop. Enhanced with crisp white, accents of sunrise yellow and sunset pink take the chill off.

Besides teaching a cool-color lesson, this room offers ideas for decorating a small space on a small budget. Whipstitch a square of fabric onto a pillow, *left*, for a quick accent. Hang a slim shelf on wooden brackets, *above*, for a low-cost table. Use a screen as a headboard; grommeted fabric panels with ribbon ties brighten this flea market find, *page 159*. (For screen how-to, see page 230.) Sew on ribbon to give pillowcases the look of costly shams, and layer fabric scraps over a round table.

To please disparate design personalities and create a cohesive scheme, pick—and name—your own unifying theme, such as "a walk in the woods." This woodland pattern in green and white works with chinked log walls to create a bucolic retreat that's rugged and romantic at the same time. The crisp contrast created by greens on white brings snappy Modern Living ambience to the otherwise dark and rustic space. Not only does the fabric's leafy pattern make a friendly nod to the earthy wood walls, but, unlike a miniprint design, the large-scale leaf motif also holds its own against the room's rugged wood surfaces. Added together, the whites of the bed fabrics and of the sheer curtains also balance the room's weighty, dark woods.

A plant in a weathered pot and a fern frond sandwiched between glass bring nature inside, echoing both the outdoor theme and color scheme.

Do you have a split design personality? You're not alone. Using nature as a link, this homeowner blended opposites: the pretty and the primitive, the light and the dark.

Color the outdoors

Isn't it time you took *your* personal style outside to play? If yours is a Modern Living personality, think of bright fabrics as adult "crayons" you can use to add fun color and pattern to bland patios and porches.

either sun nor rain can dampen the spirit of outdoor fabric accessories when you plan with easy living in mind. Portable pillows, chair pads, and tablecloths can wear the same fabrics you love indoors if you simply stow them away when not in use. A shelf in a closet or an armoire just inside the door can keep pillows and cushions close at hand for comfortable and colorful alfresco gatherings.

For totally worryfree outdoor living, consider the newest outdoor fabrics—bright, sun-resistant acrylics that look and feel like cotton. When stuffed with moisture-resistant fillings and sewn with durable polyester thread, acrylic-covered cushions and pillows can enjoy a place in the sun (or rain) all summer long. Durable tables and seating of iron, aluminum, wood, or all-weather wicker also can stand up to the elements. Now that you can relax, it's time to have some fun and plan your own colorful patio or porch redo. As you can see, chair cushions are

Artful and practical, a rugged handmade chair sets a woodsy scene on this porch. The modern edge comes from the unexpected: pastel fabrics in graphic checks and fruits.

163

just the beginning. Why not give your guests something to look up to by trimming a canvas market umbrella with friendly plaid? Or, turn bare tables into brightly welcoming settings with peppy checked cloths layered over long skirts.

se fabrics to prevent too much sunshine from cutting short a lazy afternoon on the porch or patio. In addition to making your own shade with umbrellas, consider outdoor awnings. For temporary sunshades, drape fabric over pergolas and affix with thumbtacks. You can even install rods

It's no big deal to jazz up the same old settee. Toss on comfort and color with ready-made pillows or your own custom creations. The usual pattern rules apply: Mix three scales for harmony. To create just the right palette for your outdoor living area, look around your own landscape for color cues.

and shirr on gauzy curtains to soften hard edges and fend off the sun. Such curtains are especially valuable on west-facing porches.

Thinking of your outdoor living spaces as extensions of your indoor style also opens up fresh decorating possibilities, from beautiful lighting to artful accessorizing. For starters, consider hanging a decorative candle chandelier above a dining table for light without wiring. If you spend a lot of time on a screened porch, shop for waterproof electric lamps and ceiling fans.

Soft fabrics and indoor-style accessories help you bring the style and the comfort of the indoors outside.

ccent a plain exterior wall, too. Add a wall-hung flowerpot rack, as this homeowner did. Or hang a shapely wood or iron trellis on the wall to serve as garden-style "art." An outdoor folding screen of curvy metal also can add dimension to a flat wall while providing a charming backdrop for your favorite chaise or settee.

How much simpler can outdoor decorating be? Comfy chair pads in a bright floral tie on with fat bows, candles provide light overhead, and a rack filled with flowering plants and hung on the wall works with a settee to create a focal point.

From cottage to crisp

Feeling inspired by this chapter's lively palettes and eclectic furnishings? Why not stage your own spirited decorating revival? This reborn bedroom sings the praises of happy colors and heavenly white accents.

The dreamy room you want may be only a few yards of fabric away. Here and on the following two pages, you'll see how colorful fabrics and accessories put a happy face on the same old space.

With the same basic furnishings in place, this irresistible retreat welcomes with a brighter yet more intimate feeling. What's the secret? Color! The bright floral that skirts the table shown here also covers the headboard and pillow shams to create a new scheme that blends cottage-garden charm with Modern Living spirit. Lavish doses of white add the crispness needed to make these fresh colors pop.

Besides introducing fresh color, fabric also adds decorative impact to the room by giving the bed itself newfound focal-point status. The tactic is simple: Newly made curtains tie onto dowels to frame the bed and create a snug sleeping "nook." Here, the dowels hang from large hooks screwed into the wood ceiling. If your ceiling isn't wood, simply install toggle-bolt plant hangers from which to hang slim metal or wooden rods. Plump 18-inch square pillows can make up for a missing headboard. Or, take the look to the limit, as this owner did, with an upholstered headboard. Have ¾-inch ply-

Think of the weekend place you wish you had, then decorate accordingly with cottage furniture and fun colors.

AFTER

Despite charming cottage furnishings, this room's mishmash of accessories and lack of both a focal point and a cohesive color scheme gave the space a chill, *below.* The solution was simple. First, the owner chose a charming fabric—a floral in eye-popping colors on a pale aqua-blue background—for a look that's both cottage and modern, *left.* Bright accessories, including framed pictures grouped to lend height above the headboard, repeat colors from the fabrics. Charming half-curtains topped with tie-on plaid swags take pattern to the windows without blocking valuable light. Between the windows, the original side table now imparts a fresh, airy look thanks to a coat of white paint. (For instructions to make the tabletop mirror, see pages 228–29.)

wood cut to fit your bed, then staple batting over it for softness. A fabric sleeve slips over the top and hangs loose at the bottom. Bolt the headboard to the bed frame or to the wall. The finishing touch? A clearing away of yesterday's clutter in favor of a few bright and beautiful accessories.

BEFORE

Accent your style

Whatever the shapes of things at your place, use clear colors and clutterfree backdrops to show them off.

1 Surprise, surprise! New glass vases hang on the wall, not only putting fresh blooms wherever you want them, but also giving new dimension to once-flat wallscapes.

2 Remember your geometry when you accessorize. Here, round plates make especially interesting accents when hung on a checkerboard wall. Grouped together rather than spread out around a room, such plates can help create the kind of design drama that Modern Living eyes require.

3 Star light, star bright.... A tin star becomes a sculptural element when given space to shine on an end table. In such a slick context, even apples have a colorful and shapely role to play in the scheme of things.

4 Think of table linens as accessories, too. This cloth establishes a modern background for a gathering of flowers, edibles, napkins, and luncheon plates.

5 A theme of clear colors and curvaceous lines links mismatched items, including a scalloped lampshade, vases, and a fun flower frame. Even an aging desk chair gets into the act when its beautifully bent frame is painted periwinkle blue.

6 Any shape, whether in the form of collectible pitchers like these or newly made bowls or vases, becomes "art" when two or more identically designed pieces gather together on a shelf.

7 Look for appliances to carry out a snappy kitchen scheme. Here, a colorful retro toaster echoes the bright colors and the rounded shapes of the wallcovering's fruit motifs.

8 Get the hang of personal style with a couple of cool metal shelves to support an array of objects.

9 With its up-to-date brushed-metal finish, a retro-style phone makes a functional and artful modern accent.

ow would you dress your dream bed? In rich, dark fabrics to evoke a sultan's tent or in soft, muted colors to create an oasis of tranquillity? The headboard can provide a hint of architecture. But you don't have to have the perfect bed to set your perfect style—fabric can do it for you. Use these examples as a guide. First, decide on your decorating goal—is it light, cozy, crisp, or floral? Then find the right "statement" pattern to make it happen. Using ready-made bed linens, you can change your style on a whim—say, from tailored Town and Country to flowery Beautiful Things. Or, as the first two examples show, you can create a different feeling within the same broad personality category.

Town & Country—*Light*

Elegant and clubbish, Town and Country settings can be light and bright or cozy and denlike, depending on your taste. Here, a flowing floral inspired by classic tapestries and Oriental rugs energizes the space with sunny color. Complementary plaid and airy bed curtains add a crisp, casual touch.

Town & Country—*Cozy*

In the mood to snuggle into your own lair? Hang carmel-hued curtains behind the bed, then layer bold patterns in dark colors over classic paisley and warm neutrals. For tailored sophistication, avoid fussy details, and opt for the cleaner lines of flanged shams and a bed skirt with inverted pleats.

Feel a shift of mood coming on? No problem!

Modern Living—*Crisp*

A graphic grid print in a
hand-painted style offers
a fresh, clean look. Use lots
of white for visual relief and
take full advantage of the
grid pattern to create a variety
of pillow designs and banding
for the bed skirt.

Beautiful Things—*Floral*

In this traditional style, florals
abound, but the mood is up to
you. Here, fresh pink and green
fabrics, a headboard inspired
by a garden gate, and a trellis
wallcovering evoke a cottage
garden. Buttons and bows add
a touch of romance to toss
pillows and the duvet cover.

For instant redecorating, simply change your bed linens.

inspirations beds

beautiful things
inspirations

resh, floral, romantic, pretty. Quietly refined and somewhat formal, this look takes its cue from the high-style furnishings of Colonial American merchants and landed gentry. Highly polished mahogany, walnut, and cherry are usually the woods of choice. Underfoot, Oriental or Aubusson carpets may provide the key to the room's color palette.

Elaborate window treatments based on early 20th-century Colonial Revival designs are appropriately formal in traditional rooms, but simpler treatments also may be used to lighten and refresh the look. Fabrics and wallpapers inspired by English gardens and the French countryside yield a romantic effect. Florals appear as motifs elsewhere, too—in paintings, prints, on china, in needlepoint, and in arrangements of fresh flowers in silver or crystal vases. Although the traditional style gently insists that you be on your best behavior, lively combinations of color, pattern, and accessories keep it from being staid or stuffy.

Tradition for today

One of the hallmarks of the Beautiful Things style is the theme of flowing movement inspired by nature—the motion of leaves unfurling and flowers swaying, expressing a spirit of lavish abundance.

1 t's found in the graceful curves of furniture and swagged window treatments, and even in accessories such as a silver tea service or a Baroque-style gilded mirror frame. Interpreted with a new, pared-down sensibility, Beautiful Things captures a fresh attitude toward tradition.

To the young owners of the home on the following pages, the 1950s interiors were ugly and cramped, so in one hectic summer of renovation, they began to transform them. Raising the cased openings that connected the main living areas dramatically increased the feeling of light and height. Painting boring cream walls a golden beige and the woodwork crisp white gave the rooms warmth and richness. Wood floors, liberated from wall-to-wall carpeting and refinished, enhanced the sense of space. Aluminum window frames and muntins were covered with wood molding for a classic look.

This silver tea service embodies elements of romantic traditional style: stylized C-curve foliage designs create a feeling of movement and allude to the floral inspiration of the Beautiful Things look.

To make better use of space, the couple turned the paneled den into the dining room. Painting the paneling to match the adjoining living room unites the two areas visually.

Don't forget essential details: Fringe, piping, tassels, and cording lifts furnishings, drapery, and accessories out of the ordinary.

Underscoring that visual connection, the homeowners chose a scheme of rose-red and green in a mix of florals and checks. Each room embraces the theme differently, however, so the look is unified but not slavishly matched. In the living room, a large-scale floral sets the mood, framing the windows. Gathering this fabric breaks up the pattern, but in a room with a large expanse of windows, draperies give the fabric the most play.

For a secondary print, the owners chose a coordinating medium-scale floral that condenses the color scheme in a design of overlapping tulip petals. Checked fabrics for the table skirts, a cane-sided chair, and pillows rein in the exuberance of the florals, and a solid red sofa gives the eye a tranquil place to land.

Although the coffee table injects a contemporary note with its metal frame and glass top, the curving feet and brackets echo the lines of the

Suiting the formality of Beautiful Things, gathered draperies and a swagged valance frame a wall of windows. Instead of predictable lace sheers, the owners chose sheers woven with a subtle check design for a perky, contemporary note.

swagged valance. A lattice design on the rug and a subtle check in the sheers have the same effect, refreshing
traditional style with a lively, youthful attitude.

To link the living room to the dining room, a green
diamond print used on an accent pillow reappears on

Checks and florals play well together when they share a common color scheme, *far left*. Ease the transition between the two with fringe trim. The side chair, *left*, may have a mixed pedigree stylistically, but its curving lines echo those found throughout the room. Use pillows, *page 185*, to underscore pattern themes. Treat the motif from a large-scale floral like a framed print.

the dining chairs, and a large-scale floral echoes the
rose-and-green color scheme. The dining room shows
off its traditional roots with a mix of family pieces
and reproductions. The table, built in the 1940s,
reveals its classical inspiration in the brass inlay and
fluted legs. The Empire-style chairs around it originally seated customers at a restaurant run by the
owner's grandmother on the family farm. Dating to

the 1920s or 1930s, they're solid and comfortable; dressed in flirty box-pleated skirts, they sparkle with personality.

furnishings, fabrics, and accessories that reflect well-established definitions of beauty anchor a room in the traditional style. But classic design never goes out of date. Instead, it's constantly renewed as each generation adapts and "owns" it. When tradition combines with the cleaner, lighter spaces of modern interiors, the result is formal but fresh and eminently livable.

Use one large-scale floral in a room to define its style. In adjoining rooms, you can use a different large-scale floral in each if the colors coordinate.

For an economical alternative to a wooden sideboard, the couple assembled a buffet from a plywood top and purchased legs and covered it with a corner-pleated skirt. (For instructions, see page 232.) The fabric softens the room's architecture. Simple shades downplay the windows, keeping the focus on the dining table.

Conversation clusters

Living areas are all about bringing people together. Your Beautiful Things room will make guests feel welcome if you arrange the furnishings in comfortable clusters designed to encourage conversation.

b e sure to place tables conveniently close to seating pieces so you'll have a place to put beverages, books, or magazines. Side tables should be at or near the arm level of the chairs they're partnered with so they're easy to reach. Choose antique or reproduction tables to stamp your room with the Beautiful Things style. Or for a less formal feeling, consider a brass-bound chest that does double duty as storage. Alternatively, a pair of garden urns topped with heavy glass can introduce a light, gardenlike feeling into a room filled with florals. A generously proportioned ottoman with a flat surface can hold a serving tray for snacks when it's not used for additional seating.

Resist the temptation to line the walls with furniture. Instead, pull the sofa into the room. Place a narrow table behind it or beside it to hold a lamp and accessories. Such an arrangement creates depth and interest and helps draw

A good way to anchor the seating group—and the color scheme—is with a favorite rug. The muted tones of the Aubusson rug, *page 188*, suggested the color palette. Except for accent pillows, color stays in the background for a tranquil effect.

people into the room. Because the sofa is the largest seating piece in the room, it dominates visually and serves as a natural anchor for furniture placement. Arrange side chairs or armchairs around it so they converse with each other just as your guests will. Side chairs and armchairs are more formal than upholstered club chairs, but they offer more flexibility for seating arrangements—simply pick them up and

Nurture a convivial mood by placing furniture in intimate conversational groupings. If seating pieces can "talk" to each other, so can your guests.

move them around if you need to form smaller conversational groupings when you're entertaining.

To make entrance into the conversational grouping easy, keep the path clear. Allow 2½ to 3 feet between furnishings for major traffic

For a tailored look, cover a table with a pleated skirt, *left*. Lining the pleats with the same check that covers the chair links the pieces visually. To gain maximum impact from a striped floral, *right*, gather it at the windows and show off the full repeat on a table *(left)* and chair seats *(right)*.

paths and at least 18 inches between the sofa and the coffee table and between chairs to give people room to enter the circle.

f your room feels like a listing ship when you enter it, rearrange your furniture to regain visual balance. Draw an imaginary line down the center of the room, then look at what lies on each side. Keeping things symmetrical, with similar or identical objects mirroring each other, is a no-fail way to achieve balance, but it can look stiff. To prevent this, play one large piece (like the upholstered chair on *page 192,*) off of several smaller ones (the armchairs and table).

Skirting a decorator table, *left,* is an easy way to add visual weight to part of a room and to counter the effect of too many chair and table legs. Pairing it with twin armchairs balances the hefty upholstered chair and ottoman beside the fireplace. Dressing the windows with fabric panels that look like shades adds softness without blocking light or hiding the attractive woodwork.

Position seating pieces to define the paths into and through a room, and make sure traffic doesn't cut through the center of a conversational cluster.

Forget the old rule that the sofa should be parallel to the room's focal point. Instead, place the sofa on the diagonal to open up the space and draw guests in, *left*. Fit a room for multiple tasks by proper furniture placement, *page 195*. The desk divides the space into areas for working and relaxing without making them mutually exclusive. Angling the rug leads people into the room. If you like a more ordered look, keep the rug parallel to the walls.

Around the table

To create a Beautiful Things dining room, start with the table. Polished mahogany makes the clearest traditional statement, but you can make up for the antique you wish you had with just a few yards of fabric.

1

et your chairs supply the "architecture" and define the room's style; take advantage of the fabric's pattern and color to soften and refresh the room.

If you're aiming for a formal look—or if you're covering an inexpensive decorator table—the skirt should skim the floor. (For hints on measuring the table and calculating yardage, see page 233.) Choose a plain hemmed edge for a tailored look, or trim the edge with oversize cording or a panel of ruched contrast fabric to give it more definition.

Layering cloths lets you change the room's look with the seasons or for special occasions. It's also a good way to off-set a large-scale floral. Either layer the solid-color "crumb cloth" or scarf over the floor-length patterned tablecloth, or add a floral over a solid or striped coordinating fabric (as in the breakfast room shown on *page 200*). The topper should

Dress your dining room in Beautiful Things style with classic toile on the table and walls. Unless you enjoy being totally immersed in toile, pair it with a check and a solid to keep the pattern from feeling overwhelming.

extend at least one-third of the way down the tablecloth so it doesn't look skimpy. For a casual setting, a shorter cloth is dressy without being formal. For parties and holidays, top a tablecloth with one centered runner or two placed at right angles. A solid band of color on a floral cloth gives the eye a place to rest and shows china and silverware to advantage.

If you're blessed with a handsome mahogany dining table in a traditional style, you probably won't want to cover it up, even for dining. To protect the surface from scratches and water marks, place a fabric runner down the center to showcase the centerpiece. Use place mats or cork-backed mats for the place settings.

With the table bare, consider dressing the chairs. Slipcovers

Expanses of solid color on walls and solid white on chairs and trim balance and lighten weighty, dark woods.

What could be more romantic than corsages of garden flowers attached to gauzy new "dresses" on your chairs? (For instructions, see page 234.) Assemble a centerpiece by arranging a potted orchid and flowering plants (removed from their pots) on a silver tray. Cover the roots with moss.

change the room's look for the seasons or give visual relief from so many chair and table legs.

ou can make your own slipcovers, using a commercially available pattern, and personalize them with appliqués cut from a fabric you've used elsewhere (see page 203). For a faster alternative, cover the chair backs with tabard-style covers that slip or tie in place. Tie coordinating skirted covers over the seats.

If you find a pattern you like, why not use lots of it? The blue floral at the windows, *page 200*, could stand on its own, linked by color to the stripe and miniprint wallcoverings. Adding a table topper and pillows in the same fabric gives it more emphasis. Really love the pattern? Go all out and cover walls, table, and chair seats with it, *left*. Use it at the windows, too, for an allover effect, or opt for a stripe for a touch of contrast. A sturdy country-style table like the one *above* is so versatile that it's more welcoming if left uncovered. Kids can do their homework here, the family can gather around for pizza and games, or you can put out champagne and cake for a dessert party.

Let a classic table speak for itself to assert your Beautiful Things style. This antique English pedestal table instantly establishes the room's decorating personality. Surrounding it with antique Queen Anne-style chairs suits the traditional look, but for

Don't be afraid to mix the rustic and the refined. French crystal, silverplate, and heirloom napkins convey elegance and formality. The handwoven tray, handmade dinner plate, and a whimsical salt and pepper shaker keep the table from being too serious. To underscore the garden inspiration of Beautiful Things, encase candlesticks in garden topiary forms (candles can burn beneath them).

a softer, more relaxed mood, dress the chairs with loose-fitting slipcovers. Make your own slipcovers using a commercially available pattern, or have a seamstress stitch them for you. (Interior designers have workrooms that can do the sewing for you, too.) To add a distinctive touch, appliqué a floral motif to the chair back. Here the motif came from the same fabric that's on two of the accent pillows, creating a custom-designed look. To further relax the room, an antique French daybed piled with pillows replaces chairs on one side of the table, creating a cozy setting for dining.

A sense of space

All too often, bedrooms are small, boxy spaces that give you limited options for furniture placement. In newer homes, on the other hand, the trend is toward large rooms of unbridled luxury.

Whether you find yourself sleeping in a box or a barn (figuratively speaking), you can enhance the sense of space with the help of fabric, paint, and wallpaper.

If you're blessed with an airy, spacious bedroom like the one on the following pages, revel in it. Indulge in a queen-size bed—it's comfortably in scale with the room, and 10-foot ceilings easily accommodate the height and grandeur of a classic mahogany four-poster.

To balance the bed visually and to soften the room's architecture, opt for elaborate window treatments. Floor-length draw draperies topped with swags and tails dress the windows in a formal mode, in keeping with the style of the bed. Ordinary bedside tables are likely to be too small for a queen-size four-poster bed, but a large decorator table covered with a gathered skirt offers the right scale plus plenty of room for a reading lamp, a radio or alarm clock, reading material, and family photos. Look for creative alter-

Dress the windows, the bed, and the bedside table with the same sunny floral to create a quintessential Beautiful Things bedroom. A jazzy coral and green plaid on the pillows and bed skirt (see *page 206*) accents the floral.

In a spacious bedroom,
formal draperies and swagged
valances soften the architecture
without diminishing the sense
of space. Fabric fans accented
with knotted cording cover
the gathers in the swags.
Curvaceous mirror frames,
below, evoke the
Beautiful Things style.

natives, too—a mahogany desk, for example, is the right height to stand beside the bed and turns the space in front of the window into a sunny office nook.

n this bedroom, golden yellow walls create a cheerful mood. Although warm colors typically make a space feel smaller because they appear to advance toward you, this room still feels open and airy, partly because of its ample proportions and partly because it's not overfurnished. If a sense of spaciousness is your goal, be careful not to fill every square inch with furniture.

Balance a large bed with a suitably weighty table or desk at each side, *page 206,* but don't feel compelled to fill up the room with furniture. A bench at the bed's foot serves as a handy catchall surface without crowding the room.

Painted walls may promote a more serene mood than wallpapered ones. On the other hand, if painted walls bore you, add character, texture, and depth with wallpaper. Although the rules might dictate using small prints in small spaces and large ones in

In a boxy room, covering the walls with a tiny allover pattern creates a subtle feeling of depth, *above left*. Hanging blue-and-white plates over the wallpaper enhances the effect. With the wallpaper as the smallest pattern in the room, choose fabrics that provide a variety of scales. The floral with a blue background, *above* and *page 209*, functions as a solid; a diamond-patterned floral with a white background, *page 209*, has a medium-scale motif and an airy effect; the third, a floral stripe on the duvet, tables, and shams, offers the largest scale. To keep blue and white from being too chilly, add doses of warm yellow.

grander ones, you can bend the rules if you know what effect you want to achieve. Papering a small bedroom with a large-scale floral, for example, makes the space feel like a cocoon. Stripes lift the eye to the ceiling, emphasizing the illusion of height. Small checks or dainty overall designs may nearly disappear, creating a quiet look.

Experts used to say "choose one statement print plus four little go-withs"—but no more. Instead, choose seven or eight different patterns and tie them all together with color.

No four-poster bed in your house? Add character and height to the bedroom with lace curtains hung around the head of the bed, *left*. Hang the fabric panels on rods suspended from the ceiling with eye hooks. (See page 169 for tips on creating a similar treatment.) Emphasize the bed with a symmetrical grouping of objects on the wall above it, *center*. The painting provides a focal point, framed by the arrangement of plates. Don't hang the painting too high—your eye should be able to connect it to the bed easily. In a small, oddly shaped room, *right*, using the same large-scale pattern on walls, windows, and furnishings may actually enlarge the sense of space. The room's angles and edges seem to melt away behind the screen of florals. Installing the cornice near the ceiling raises the apparent height of the window, which further enhances the illusion of roominess.

In a small master bath, *left*, play up the light and open up the space visually with pale neutral tiles and a wallpaper with barely-there color and pattern. The wallpaper-covered cornice is easy to make from plywood (see page 231 for instructions). A modified balloon shade adds softness and can be dropped for privacy. Dainty allover patterns applied to walls, windows, and furnishings in a master bath suite, *page 213*, create a distinctly feminine feeling. Anchor it with larger-scale pattern (supplied here by the border and rug) and areas of solid color. A neat stripe inside the bookshelves keeps the overall effect from being too saccharine.

Which colors and patterns make you feel serene? Light colors and quiet patterns like those shown here help you start your day gently and end it with tranquillity.

Blurring the boundaries

Furnishing a screen or covered porch or open patio with comfortable seating, plump cushions, and tables covered with gathered skirts turns the space into a fresh-air room.

On a screen porch, where furnishings will be protected from the weather, use the same fabrics that you would use indoors for chair cushions, pillows, and table skirts. For outdoor use, it's best to choose cushions covered with acrylic fabrics. Acrylics feel like cotton but resist fading, mold, and mildew and can be cleaned easily with soap and water. If you can't find the colors and patterns you want in ready-mades, stitch your own pillows and tablecloths from acrylics. Look for the weatherproof fabrics in home sewing centers, and remember to use polyester thread when sewing them. It's more durable than cotton thread.

Before the recent improvements in acrylics, laminated cottons offered the best option for outdoor cushions and tablecloths. A vinyl coating on the fabrics prevents mildewing, fading, and rotting. Laminates are still available, and

Floral fabrics turn a covered porch into a romantic spot for entertaining and relaxing. Protect cottons from rain and high humidity. For weatherproof soft furnishings, choose acrylic fabrics, sold under names such as Sun 'N Shade™.

you can laminate your own fabric, too, using an iron-on vinyl coating from a fabric store. The drawback, however, is that water can seep in through the stitching holes and eventually ruin the fabric. If you do choose laminates, use nylon/polyester thread.

o dress an outdoor room, choose patterns and colors that blend with the surroundings. Shades of blue and green create a visual connection to the tree-shaded lawn outside and act as a cooling counterpoint to a sunnier exposure. If your garden blooms in summer-long color, consider keying your fabrics to the hues of flowers outdoors.

Cover a folding screen with fabric and use it to hide the inevitable clutter of toys and garden tools on a screen porch. Use the same fabric on chair and bench cushions to pull the room together visually. For a dressy look, slip a fitted top over a skirted table (see pages 232 and 233 for tips on making table skirts).

Outdoor living

Turning your patio into a party spot is easier than ever with new acrylic fabrics that withstand dampness and strong sunlight. For special occasions, enrich the mix with accessories made from cotton.

pillows, tablecloths, and napkins all can be stitched from washable cotton coordinates that work with the weatherproof textiles. You even can spiff up a market umbrella (available from hardware stores) with a tie-in liner, giving it the feeling of a tent. (The cotton items must come indoors for the night, since they could be damaged by dew or rain.)

To give herself more options, this homeowner had the tie-on chair pads made with two coordinating acrylic fabrics so they'd be reversible. This lets her combine them with different tablecloths and linens; the floral side looks sunny and bright for a breakfast or luncheon, while the plaid suits an alfresco dinner.

For a party or other special occasion, the tablecloth need not be weatherproof. A full skirt brings much-needed softness to a severe setting dominated by brick and iron. It also gives the table visual weight and provides a focal point for the patio

A gathered skirt with a floral topper transforms an ordinary iron table into an elegant dining spot. (See pages 233–34 for instructions to make a tablecloth for an umbrella-shaded patio table.)

grouping (although in this setting, the real focal point is the view). If you like the impact of the skirted table, however, choose acrylic fabrics so you can enjoy the effect all season long. In choosing fabrics, consider bolder patterns and colors than you might be comfortable with indoors. They won't seem overpowering in full sun.

BEFORE

AFTER

Treat contemporary iron furniture as a neutral background for romantic-looking fabrics. Skirting the table creates instant personality.

Liven up ordinary patio furniture, *above*, with cushions made from acrylic fabrics and accessories stitched from coordinating cottons. A pink plaid cotton with a seersucker weave, *page 220, top left*, is reversible so it works well for napkins. Reversible tie-on chair pads, *page 220, top right*, let you change the look with a mere flip of the cushion. An interior designer's workroom can customize a standard market umbrella with a tie-in liner, *page 220, bottom left*. Here, a 30-inch-deep band of fabric ties to the spokes and the tips of the ribs. The comfy, full-length cushion on the hammock, *page 220, bottom right*, is weatherproof, but bring the pillows in for the night.

Accent your style

If you're a Beautiful Things personality, you'll love accessories like these. Look for similar kinds of objects to bring the style home.

1 Antique or reproduction Staffordshire dogs, Oriental porcelain lamps, and Waterford crystal are staples of the Beautiful Things style, which is rooted in English and French decorative traditions.

2 Look for antique or reproduction porcelain plates and hang them in a symmetrical pattern on the wall. Antique tea caddies and wooden boxes serve decorative and practical storage purposes.

3 Antique boxes like this lady's writing desk do butler duty when displayed chairside on a small bench or custom-made table. The silver filigree tray on top holds antique inkwells.

4 Floral-patterned needlepoint or wool rugs put Beautiful Things style underfoot.

5 Floral paintings in an old-master style can be purchased through interior decorators, or you can buy reproductions of museum originals and

hang them in carved, gilded frames. Silver pieces for entertaining, such as goblets, trays, and pitchers, express traditional formality.

6 Painted furniture like this armoire and a novelty lamp with a bow-embellished lampshade show off the softer side of Beautiful Things.

7 Mother-of-pearl handles distinguish this collection of antique and new silver serving pieces and flatware. Even accessories such as a magnifying glass

fit the collection since all are unified by the pearl handles.

8 Create a tablescape of Oriental and English porcelains, ceramic objects, and books, varying their heights for interest. The monkey statue recalls British Colonial style.

9 Framed parrot prints suggest the look of 18th-century illustrations by artist-naturalists. Accessories include antique English glass jars on stands and a Venetian glass candy dish.

inspirations *your* workroom

Projects for home decorating

Whether you're a do-it-yourselfer or prefer to hire professional assistance, here's information you need to help you get the job done right.

get started by choosing the right fabric for your purposes. Shopping for decorator fabrics presents a bewildering array of choices. How do you know what to buy?

Fabric companies group textiles into three categories: upholstery weight, multipurpose, and lightweight. To be placed in a given category, fabric must pass a variety of tests, including tensile strength, tear strength, abrasion resistance, and lightfastness.

Upholstery fabrics have the highest tensile strength, tear strength, and resistance to abrasion—they're sturdy enough to stand up to repeated use as you sit on them or lean against them. Multipurpose fabrics are lighter in weight and slightly less resistant to rubbing or abrasion; use them for upholstery that won't receive hard wear as well as for draperies, slipcovers, pillows, and table skirts. The lightweight fabrics are recommended only for drapery because they don't resist abrasion well. You can use these fabrics for slipcovers or pillow shams for special effects, but they won't hold up to daily wear and tear the way heavier fabrics will.

Upholstery fabrics for residential use (as opposed to commercial grades for hotels and restaurants) are not treated for flame retardance, but your interior designer can send yardage out for treatment for you. Most upholstery-weight fabrics, however, meet standards set by the Upholstered Furniture Action Council to prevent their igniting from cigarette burns. In addition, some fibers, such as wool and certain synthetic fibers, are self-extinguishing. Cotton and polyester/cotton blends, however, are flammable.

Many upholstery- and medium-weight fabrics are treated at the factory with a silicone treatment that protects them from stains and soil. This information is printed on the selvage of the fabric. If the material you want to use hasn't been treated, ask your interior designer to send it out for treatment, or apply a spray yourself. The factory-applied coating provides better protection. If you do it yourself, you'll need to reapply the spray after each cleaning.

To care for upholstery and draperies, vacuum them regularly to remove dust. When cleaning is necessary, have draperies and slipcovers professionally dry-cleaned rather than washing them. The process is gentler on the fibers and helps colors last longer.

past perfect

Making a Stencil (see page 58)

To make your own stencil, choose a motif with simple lines and few details. Photocopy or trace the design on paper, then lay a sheet of stencil plastic (from a crafts store) over the paper. Using a permanent marking pen, trace the outlines of the design, then trace interior lines that help define the shape. Remember that whatever you cut away is where color will go, so you'll need to leave bridges or connecting strips to hold the stencil together and to divide areas of color.

Using a crafts knife with a new blade, cut out the areas that will be painted. It's best to work on a cutting mat, but you can use a magazine or a piece of cardboard instead; just discard it after cutting one stencil.

To apply the stencil paint, use masking tape or stencil adhesive to secure the stencil to the surface. Dip the brush in stencil paint, then wipe the brush on a paper towel to remove the excess paint. Starting at the edges of the cutout area and working toward the center, apply the paint with a circular motion. Or, if you prefer a stippled look, apply the paint with a dabbing motion. Let the paint cure according to the manufacturer's instructions; protect the surface with a spray varnish.

making a stencil

daybed canopy

Daybed Canopy (see page 75)

To hold the fabric over the bed, you'll need a 1-inch-diameter dowel or drapery rod, a finial for drapery rods, and an oval or round wooden plaque (from a crafts store). Cut the dowel to 18 to 24 inches long. Screw the finial into one end of the dowel and use a wood screw to attach the plaque to the other end. Paint the entire unit as desired; mount the plaque on the wall using screws and wall anchors.

To make the canopy, measure from the floor at one end of the bed up to the canopy pole and down to the floor at the other end of the bed. Cut fabric and lining to this length. To make the scalloped border, cut two 5-inch-wide strips from one long edge of the fabric. To make a template for the scallops, use a piece of poster board; draw a line 4 inches from one long edge, then use a saucer or bread plate to draw half circles along the line. Cut out along the half circles. Pin the fabric strips together, right sides facing. Place the template on the wrong side of the fabric and draw the scallops, then stitch along the drawn line. Clip the curves and turn.

Trim the lining to the same width as the remaining width of fabric. Pin the scalloped strip to one long edge of the fabric, right sides facing and raw edges aligned. Pin the lining to the fabric, right sides facing and with the scalloped strip sandwiched in between. Stitch around all edges, leaving an opening at the back for turning. Turn, press, and arrange over the hanging rod.

town&country

Raising a Bed (see page 110)

To raise a twin bed so it has the height of a daybed, raise it on a frame of 2x4s. Measure the metal bed frame to determine the lengths required. Plan on two 2x4s to run the length of the bed, then cut three 2x4s to fit crosswise between them. Use wood glue and wood screws to attach the crosswise slats to the lengthwise boards. Place the frame on the bed frame and place the mattress on top.

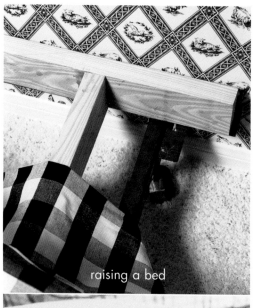

raising a bed

modern living

Slipcovered Ottoman
(see page 132)

slipcovered ottoman

Materials: fabric, ball fringe, thread to match, quilt batting (optional)

Make the slipcover in two parts, top and skirt. For the top, measure from the "waist" (just above the middle of the ottoman side), across the top, and down to the waist of the opposite side. Cut a circle of fabric this diameter plus 1 inch for seam allowances (see Tips for Making a Tablecloth on page 233). Center the fabric circle on top of the ottoman, wrong side up, and pin-fit it around the sides by making small single pleats or tucks. Baste the pleats in place.

For the skirt, measure from the "waist" to the floor for the depth and add 1 inch for seam allowances. To determine the length you'll need, measure the circumference of the ottoman. Determine how far apart you want the pleats, then divide that number into the circumference to get the number of pleats that will fit. Multiply the number of pleats by 4 inches (for 2-inch-deep pleats); add the resulting figure to the circumference for the amount of fabric you'll need for the skirt. Piece as necessary to obtain a strip this long.

Pin box pleats in place and baste to hold. Check the fit of the skirt around the ottoman, then stitch the short ends of the skirt. Join the top to the skirt, then topstitch ball fringe over the seam.

If your ottoman has a buttoned, tufted top, cover it with quilt batting to smooth out the surface. Cut the batting to fit the top of the ottoman, then pull the slipcover over the ottoman.

Vanity Mirror (see page 170)
Materials: ⅛-inch birch plywood; jigsaw; 8x10 wood

228

picture frame and mirror to fit; spray primer; white latex spray paint; white, pink, and bright blue acrylic crafts paints; wood glue; finish nails; silk rose; ribbon; latex glazing liquid; hot-glue gun and glue sticks; hinge

On the plywood, draw off a 15x21-inch rectangle. On one short edge (the top) round the corners and draw a gently curving top. (Use a dinner plate to guide you if you're not confident about drawing freehand.) Cut out the shape with a jigsaw. Also cut a stand that measures 13 inches tall, 3 inches wide at the top, and 6 inches wide at the bottom.

On the plywood, mark the position for the mirror, centering it on the shape. Cut out an opening the same size as the mirror. Spray the plywood rectangle and stand with primer, then with white paint. Thin the blue paint with the glazing liquid and, using a narrow sponge brush or a 1-inch-wide paintbrush, paint stripes as shown, *top*.

Prime the 8x10-inch picture frame, then paint it pink. For an aged look, mix white acrylic crafts paint with glazing liquid, then wipe it over the frame. Attach the frame over the opening in the plywood rectangle by nailing it with finish nails from the back.

Use hot glue to attach the gingham ribbon and rose as shown. Attach the stand to the back with a small

vanity mirror

overdoor shelf and valance

hinge. Insert the mirror, securing it with the clips that come with the picture frame.

Overdoor Shelf (see page 134)
Materials: two 10x10 pine corbels with embedded hanging slot (from a home-improvement center), 1x10 pine board, router (or decorative molding and finish nails), drill and drill bits, screws, latex paint in desired color

Cut the pine board to the desired length. To finish the edges, either use a router to trim the edges, or attach decorative molding with wood glue and finish nails. Attach the shelf to the tops of the corbels with screws, making sure the back edge of the shelf is flush with the back edge of the corbel. Paint the unit the desired color. Install the mounting screws (which come with the corbels) in the wall, following the manufacturer's instructions. If possible, install the corbels beside the door or window woodwork or in a stud so they're securely braced. Fit the corbel hanging slots over the screws.

Valance
Materials: fabric, thread to match, drapery cable cord and metal clamps, drill and drill bits, S hooks, curtain rings with clips (available at home-decorating stores and through home-decorating catalogs)

229

For the valance, cut and piece fabric as necessary to obtain two strips 1½ times the length of the shelf. For the width, measure from the shelf to the door or window frame and add 1 inch for seam allowances. Stitch the two strips together along the bottom edge, right sides facing, following the edge of a motif (the banana on this fabric resulted in a scalloped edge). Trim the excess fabric and clip any curves. Stitch the top and side edges, leaving an opening for turning. Turn and press.

Drill a hole through each shelf bracket near the top corner. Push one end of the drapery cable through each hole and secure it on the outside of the bracket with a metal clamp. Use S hooks and the clip rings to attach the valance.

Folding Screen (see page 159)

Materials: wooden or metal folding screen, fabric, thread to match, large grommets and grommet tool, ribbon to match fabrics

Cut the fabric to fit the screen openings, adding 3 inches at the top and bottom and 1 inch at each side. Fold all raw edges under, then fold again, making a 1½-inch hem at the top and bottom and a ½-inch hem on each side. Topstitch the hems in place.

Insert grommets evenly across the top and bottom

folding screen

fabric rug

edges, centering them in the hems. Tie the panels to the screen's cross bars with ribbon. You can let the bottom edges float freely, or stretch the fabric panels tightly and tie them in place.

Fabric Rug (see page 140)

Materials: main fabric for rug, contrasting fabric for border, threads to match, dressmaker's chalk, thin fleece batting

Cut two pieces of the main fabric to the desired size. To make sure the corners are square and the ends of the rug straight, use at least one selvage as one side of the rug. Align a book (or a T-square or a right-angle template) with the selvage and draw a line across the top of the book. If you use the full width of the fabric, repeat this procedure on the other side, then connect the lines and cut straight across. (If your rug is narrower than the full width of the fabric, use a straightedge to measure from the selvage to the desired width at two points; connect these points to draw off the second long side, then mark the short ends as directed above.) Repeat to mark and cut the remaining short end.

For the border strips, first determine the desired finished border width, double it, and add 1 inch for seam allowances. For the long side borders, cut the strip the same length as the rug plus 1 inch.

For the short side borders, cut the strip the length of the short side plus twice the finished width of the border.

Stitch the long side borders to the long sides of one rug piece, right sides facing; open out the borders and press the seams. Stitch the short end borders to the short sides and border strips. Open out and press the seams, then lay the piece wrong side up.

Smooth the fleece batting over the entire rug, extending it into the borders. If necessary, join two widths of batting with zigzag stitches. Pin the remaining rug piece over the batting, wrong side down, making sure edges are even and the fabric is smooth. Starting in the middle of one long side and working toward the corners, fold the border in half; then fold the raw edge under, encasing both rug pieces and the batting. Pin the

fabric border rug

wallpaper-covered cornice

border in place, smoothing the fabric and easing the border to fit. Repeat for the remaining long side, then repeat for the short sides. Trim excess fabric in the corners, if necessary, to reduce bulk. Topstitch all borders in place, stitching close to the folded edge; this will catch the batting and both pieces of the main fabric so the batting won't slip or shift between the fabric layers.

Fabric Border for Sisal Rug
(see page 135)

Materials: fabric for border, hot-glue gun and glue sticks, purchased sisal rug

Cut strips of fabric the desired length and width of the borders plus 1 inch all around. Press all raw edges under ½ inch. Glue the border strips to the sisal rug, overlapping the strips at each corner.

beautiful things

Wallpaper-Covered Cornice
(see page 212)

Materials: ⅜-inch plywood, jigsaw, 2x4s, wood screws, white interior paint, wallpaper, white glue, sharp utility knife, ball fringe, angle brackets

Cut the plywood to the desired size. This cornice extends about 2 inches beyond the window frame on each side and measures about one-third the height of the window. To draw the scallops, divide the width by four, then divide that measurement in half for the half-scallops at the ends. Use a jigsaw to cut out the scallops.

From the 2x4s, cut two lengths equal to the sides of the plywood piece. Cut a third length to fit along the top. Screw the top and sides of the plywood piece to the narrow edges of the 2x4s for mounting on the wall.

Paint the entire piece white, then glue wallpaper to the front of the plywood. After the glue dries, turn the piece facedown and trim the wallpaper along the scalloped edge, using a utility knife. Use glue to attach the fringe along the scalloped edge. Mount the cornice on the wall, using angle brackets.

Skirted Buffet Table
(see page 186)

Materials: ½-inch plywood cut to desired size for tabletop, four unfinished 32-inch turned legs fitted with screws (from a home-improvement center), two 2x4s, wood screws, drill and drill bits, fabric and lining to cover table, cording for piping, 6-inch-deep fringe, thread to match fabric

From the 2x4s, cut two lengths about 6 inches shorter than the table's long sides. Standing each 2x4 on its narrow side, position each about 4 inches in from the tabletop's

skirted buffet table

fitted table topper

long edges, centered between the short ends. Attach the 2x4s with wood screws. Attach the screw plates for the turned legs to the 2x4s, then screw the legs in place.

For the table skirt top, measure the tabletop and add ½ inch all around for seam allowances; cut fabric and lining to this size. For the skirt, measure the width of one side by the height of the table; add 2¾

inches at each side for 2¾-inch-deep pleats and ½ inch all around for seam allowances. Measure the width of the front by the height of the table; add 8¼ inches at each side (for a 2¾-inch-deep pleat and turning the corner) and a ½-inch seam allowance all around. This should position the seams inside the side pleats. Cut two side pieces and a front and a back to these measurements from both the lining and the fabric. Baste the lining to the wrong side of each piece, then stitch the panels together; pin and baste the pleats.

Cover the cording with fabric to make piping. Stitch the piping to the top, then join the skirt to the top. Turn under a ½-inch hem along the skirt's bottom edge and topstitch fringe over the hem.

Fitted Table Topper
(see page 217)

To make a simpler version of this fitted topper, measure the diameter of the tabletop, and add 1 inch for seam allowances. Cut a circle of fabric and of lining this size. For the drop, measure around the tabletop, and add 1 inch for a seam allowance; also measure the depth of the drop (it should be about one-third the distance from the tabletop to the floor), and add 1 inch for the hem. Cut strips of fabric and lining to these dimensions. To scallop the edge, use a compass or a plate to draw scallops along one edge of the fabric strip and the lining.

To assemble the skirt, pin piping to the right side of the fabric along the scalloped edge, with raw edges aligned, then pin the lining over the piping. Stitch close to the piping. Clip curves and turn the strip right side out. Stitch the short ends together, right sides of the fabric facing, forming a tube. Turn right side out.

Stitch piping to the edge of the fabric circle. Pin, then stitch the fabric circle to the scalloped tube, with right sides of the fabric facing.

Tips for making a round or oval tablecloth

For a floor-length round tablecloth, measure the tabletop from edge to edge; measure the drop, or distance from the tabletop to the floor, and double it. Add the two figures, plus 2 to 4 inches for the hem. The resulting sum will be the size of the fabric square from which you'll need to cut the circle.

If you need to piece fabric to get the required size square, cut two lengths of fabric the measurement of the square. Cut one length in half lengthwise, and stitch one half to each side of the remaining length.

To cut the square into a circle, fold the fabric in half, then in half again so it's quartered. Pin one end of

round or oval tablecloth

patio tablecloth with umbrella hole

a piece of string to the folded center. Tie a piece of dressmaker's chalk or a pencil to the other end; the string length should equal the radius (half the diameter) of the tablecloth, including the hem. Keeping the string taut, swing the chalk across the cloth from corner to corner, marking off a curve. Cut along this line.

For an oval tablecloth, measure the length and width of the tabletop from edge to edge. Add the length of the top to twice the length of the drop, plus 4 inches for the hem. Then add the width of the top to twice the length of the drop, plus 4 inches for the hem. These measurements will give you the size of the rectangle of fabric you'll need. Fold the fabric in quarters and trim the free (unfolded) edges in a curve to make an oval.

Patio Tablecloth with Umbrella Hole (see page 221)

Materials: fabric, thread to match

For the tablecloth top, measure the diameter of the tabletop. Cut a fabric circle to this size plus 1 inch for seam allowances (see Tips for Making a Round or Oval Tablecloth).

Using a plastic template (available from office-supply stores and art stores) and a pencil, draw a 2-inch-diameter circle (or a circle large enough to accommodate your umbrella pole) at the center of the tablecloth top, centering the circle over the marked center point. From a fabric scrap, cut an 8-inch diameter circle for the umbrella-hole facing. With the plastic template, draw a 2-inch diameter circle at the center of the facing. Place the facing on the tablecloth top, right sides facing, lining up the drawn circles. Stitch over the pencil line.

Clip through both fabrics at the center of the circle, then cut a quarter-size hole in the center of the stitched circle. Clip the curves of the seam allowance, then turn the facing to the underside of the tablecloth (*above right*). Press.

To make the gathered skirt, cut eight panels the width of the fabric and 32 inches long (or the height of your tabletop). Join the panels at the sides to make a large tube. Hem the bottom edge. Gather the top edge in 24-inch sections. Adjust the gathers to fit the tabletop piece. Stitch the skirt to the top, right sides facing.

To make the square table topper, cut a square, using the full width of the fabric. Hem the edges. Make a faced hole in the center as for the tablecloth.

Chair Corsage (see page 198)

Materials: chemistry vial or test tube, 3-inch-wide wire mesh ribbon, fine crafts wire, large-eye needle,

patio tablecloth umbrella-hole facing

chair corsage

polymer clay (from a crafts store), 1-inch-wide French wire-edge ribbon

Cut a piece of 3-inch-wide mesh ribbon the length of the vial. Wrap it around the vial, overlapping the edges at the back. Using the fine crafts wire and large-eye needle, stitch the edges together and gather the bottom.

From the polymer clay, shape a teardrop bead. Make a loop from the crafts wire and insert it into the top of the bead, then bake according to the manufacturer's instructions. (If the clay shrinks slightly during baking, the wire may pull out, so apply a drop of clear-drying crafts glue to the base of the loop after the bead cools.) Wire the bead to the bottom of the mesh sleeve.

Cut three 7-inch lengths of 1-inch-wide French wire-edge ribbon. Using the needle, work the mesh ribbon threads apart to make three small openings, evenly spaced, around the top of the sleeve. Push a piece of ribbon through each opening and cut the ends at an angle. Arrange the ribbons so they suggest leaves around the base of the bouquet.

Use the fine crafts wire to make a loop at the top of the sleeve to hook over the button on the slipcover. For your party, fill the vial half full with water and insert flowers.

inspirations resources

See a fabric or a design you love? Here's where to go for more information.

Note: Fabrics and wallpapers shown in this book were available from Waverly as of the date of publication. Items may be discontinued without notice; if a fabric or wallpaper you like is no longer available, call consumer information at 800/423-5881 for help in finding a substitute.

For more information on Waverly fabric, wallpaper, or Home Store locations, visit Waverly's web site at www.decoratewaverly.com. Or call 800/423-5881. For information on Waverly paint, call 800/631-3440. In addition to ready-made bed linens and accessories, Waverly offers a made-to-order service called Selections; you can choose from more than 150 fabrics and a variety of window and bed treatments; the Waverly workroom fabricates them for you and delivers them to your home. Visit the Web site for complete details.

Page 3: photographer: William P. Steele.

Page 7: bed hangings: Briar Rose/Lemongrass 664563; daybed cover: Rosebank/Lemongrass 664555; pillows: Greenwich/Lemongrass 647285, Wellesley/Lemongrass 647275, Rosebank/Lemongrass 647553, Nichole/Linen 647350, Nichole Check/Linen 647360.

Page 8: chair: Romeo/Lilac 647230; wallpaper: Garden Lane Companion/Sky 571790; duvet cover: Cambria/Aquamarine 663364; bedskirt: Brilliant/Bluebell 602126; bed hangings: Carre/Pool 615043; bed linens: by Waverly.

Page 14: left: accessories, Waverly Home; headboard, Hans/Oyster 664062; Inga bedding ensemble from The Luxury Collection by Waverly; comforter and shams: Inga; Eurosham: Stockholm Stripe; solid pillow: Emma; right: see page 101.

Page 15: left: sofa, pillows: Chubby Check/Cobalt 663612; draperies: Precious Posies/Cobalt 663582; club chair, pillows: Misty Meadow/Cobalt 663592; chair, window shades, pillow: Slender Stripe/Cobalt 663602; pillows: Cheery Cherries/Cobalt 663572; welt: Limerick/Sunshine 647102 solid pillows: Glosheen/Bluebell 645531; right:, see Page 7.

Page 18: wallpaper: Pageantry Scroll/Buttercream 573012, Pageantry Stripe/Buttercream 573022, Grandeur Texture/Parchment 573030, Pageantry Border/Buttercream 573002; pillows: Pageantry/Buttercream 663872, Greenwich/Lemongrass 647285, Dresden/Buttercream 663892; bed linens: by Waverly.

Page 19: right: color Jewel; chairs: Castille 663752; ottoman: Aragon 663742; windows: Villa 663732.

Page 20: wallpaper: color Sunwashed; Pairs of Pears 574242, Checkmate 574635; border: Fruit Salad Border 574192; window shade: Block Party 664205.

Pages 21 and 124: wallpaper: Langston Stripe/Chambray 571128, Whitworth/Parisian 569830;

border: Langston Border/Chambray 571111; chair, pillow, draperies: Gazelle/Royale 600115; pillow piping: Bryant/Atlantic 600055; drapery (reverse): Beaumont/Atlantic 600153; pillow: Jester/Currant 600001.

Page 22: color Cotton Candy; wallpaper: Precious Posies Bouquet 572581, Slender Stripe Companion 572671; border: Precious Posies Border 572601; windows: Precious Posies 663581, Slender Stripe 663601; pillows: Cheery Cherries 663571, Chubby Check 663611.

Page 23: sofa, pillow: Romance/Scarlet 663450; upholstered chair, ottoman, table skirt, sofa pillows: Spring Song/Scarlet 663460; draperies, chair pillow: Enchantress/Scarlet 663440; solid sofa pillows: Ranger/Chestnut 630003.

Page 24: sofa: Izmir/Onyx 664591; windows, ottoman: Minaret/Onyx 664601; chairs: Silk Strié/Onyx 664611; pillows: Newport/Onyx 667292, Silk Strié/Khaki 664615.

Page 25: wallpaper: Baltic Brocade/Oyster 573602; sofa: Greta/Copen 664070; chair: Nicholas Plaid/Copen 664020; valance: Stockholm Stripe/Copen 647264; sheers: Inga/Ecru L143-141-4284.

Page 28: left: drapery, pillows: Montague/Parchment 664280; chair: Foularde/Claret 664312; sofa: Capulet/Willow 647317; table skirt: Capulet Stripe/Parchment 664290 ; right: wallpaper: Garden Leaf/Lime 572190, Waterman Stripe/Cobalt 572253; border: Gardener's Border/Lime 572180; bench pad, valance, apron: Pastoral Plaid/Grass 663534; pillows: Playful Plaid/Grass 603003, McCheck/Blue 608020.

Page 29: left: color Topaz; wallpapers: Lynnbrook 572793, Penrose Companion 572824, Lynnbrook Border 572803, Penrose Border 572814; windows, chair: Lynnbrook 663723; ottoman, pillow: Prescott 663685; right: wallpaper: Florida/Cobalt 574101, Florida Border/Cobalt 574011; sink skirt: Simple Stripe/Cherry 664423.

Page 32: top: wallpaper: Falling Leaves/Leaf 572484, Picket Fences Border/Sunshine 572432; chair, pillow: Playful Plaid/Sunshine 603004; pillow: Charming Check/Sunshine 602994; bottom: wallpaper: color Black; Merry Cherry 572405, Waterman Stripe 572258, Merry Cherry Border 572413; pillows: Pick Me/Cherry 663141, McCheck/Black 608025, McCheck/Red 608023.

Page 33: top: chair, tablecloth: Bremen/Tapestry 663911; wallpaper: Salzburg Companion/Crimson 572991; bottom, see page 120.

Page 34: wall screen: Pageantry/Sage 663871; chair: Swanhurst/Sage 647255; sofa, chaise, pillows: Prague/Celery 663884; pillows: Prague/Plum 663881.

Page 35: sofa: Prague/Plum 663881; chair, pillow: Swanhurst/Sage 647255; drapery: Dresden/Sage 663891; table skirt, pillow: Pageantry/Sage 663871; table topper: Limerick/Antique 647093; window shade, pillows: Perfection/Beige 647193.

Pages 36–37: See pages 52 and 140.

Page 38: upholstered chair: Shelburne/Barn Red 663321; pillow: Meeting House/Barn Red

663291; drapery: New Hope/Indigo 663310; chair slipcovers: Thornhill/Barn Red 647171; table topper: Farmstead/Federal 663251; trim: Limerick/Chambray 647115.

Page 39: upholstered headboard, pillow: Brilliant/Lemon 602123; coverlet, draperies, pillow shams: Garden Lane/Sky 663390; coverlet reverse: Pretty Petals/Sky 663400; table skirt, bed pillow: Northport/Lemonade 601492; pillow on bed: No. 9 Ferns-Print Shoppe/Butter 663552.

Pages 42, 58–59: color Clay; settee: Stockholm Stripe 647263; pillows: Eugenia 664001, Inga 664031, Hans 664061; cocktail ottoman: Greta 664071; chair (pair): Helena 664041; welting: Limerick 647105; chair (foreground): Fredrik 663991; folding screen: Baltic Brocade 664051; mantel scarf: Swedish Arbor 664081; trim: Nicholas Plaid 664021.

Pages 44–51: designer: Deborah Hastings, Birmingham, Ala.; stylist: Phyllis Murell; photographer: Emily Minton. Rug: Waverly Home, Atlanta; settee cushion, chair back cushions: Bremen/Hunter 663910; settee pillows: Ottoman/Leaf 647023, piping, chair seat cushions: General Store/Fern 662782; draperies: Lowe/Natural 370340; sofa: Inga/Copen 664030, cushions Jacqueline/Pumpkin 600899; wicker chair: Swedish Arbor 664080; club chair, ottoman: Wellington/Laurel 661430, Eugenia/Clay 664001, Hans/Oyster 664062, Country Fair/Mulberry 662680.

Pages 52–54: color Sage; window: Simple Stripe 664425, Country Fair 647433; sofa, chair, pillows: Last Summer 664351; pillows: Field of Flowers 647423, Summer Stripe 664361.

Pages 56–57: color Mulberry except as noted; drapery, sofa: Lookout Mountain Vintage 662223; chair cushion, pillow, table skirt: Hillsdale Vintage 662600; pillows: Wall Street 662715, Pantry Plaid 662670, Grand Teton 662790, Heirloom Ticking/Sage 662751; upholstered chair: Sweet Violets Vintage 662491.

Pages 60–61: wallpaper: Langston Stripe/Crimson 571123, Fairhaven/Rose 570923, Norfolk Rose Border/Rose 570860, Bows Jolie Border/Crimson 563666; sofa, chair cushion: Norfolk Rose/Rose 662510; piping: Country Fair/Crimson 662682; windows, pillow: Fairhaven/Rose 662623; upholstered chair, pillow, window shades: General Store/Crimson 662780 pillows: Fernwood Vintage/Crimson 662642.

Pages 62–63: color Oyster; curtains: Inga 664032; chair, ottoman: Baltic Brocade 664052; pillows: Gustavian Stripe 664012, Fredrik 663992; trim: Hans 664062. Patterns:Butterick.

Pages 64–69: designer: Rhea Crenshaw, Rhea Crenshaw Interiors, Memphis, Tenn.; stylist: Julie Azar; photographer: Emily Minton; workroom: Unique Decor, Memphis, Tenn.; wallpaper: Pantry Plaid/Blush 570961; valance, window seat cushion, chair cushions: Charade Vintage/Crimson 662550; shade and pillows: Country Fair/Citron 662687; dining room draperies: Highgrove/Topaz 647243; slipcovers: Hans/Clay 664061.

Page 70: comforter, pillows, drapery, chair: Norfolk Rose/Rose 662510; comforter, dust ruffle, pillows, chair: Fairhaven/Rose 662623; dust ruffle, pillows, drapery, and chair: General Store/Crimson 662780; pillow: Country Fair/Canvas 662683.

Pages 72–73: comforter, draperies, valance, pillow shams, table topper: Lucinda/Citron 662450; comforter reverse, dust ruffle, pillow shams: General Store/Fern 662782; table skirt: Fernwood Vintage/Fern 662645; pillows: Country Fair/Fern 662685.

Pages 74–75: color Oyster except as noted; ottoman, scarf trim: Stockholm Stripe 647260; chair, pillows: Inga 664032, Nicholas Plaid 664022; coverlet, pillows: Baltic Brocade 664052; pillows, scarf: Hans 664062, Eugenia 664002; canopy: Greta 664072, Gustavian Stripe 664012; shades: Fredrik 663992; sheers: Caprice/Cream 631302.

Page 76–77: wallpaper: Sweet Violets Vintage Toss/Blush 571090; Langston Stripe/Violet 571120; border: Sweet Violets Vintage Border/Blush 570940; comforter, pillows: Sweet Violets Vintage/Blush 662490; piping: Country Fair/Sage 662686; chair: Old Lyme Vintage/Sage 662612; pillows, bed skirt: Fernwood Vintage/Sage 662641; windows, pillow: Pantry Plaid/Blush 662671, Old Lyme Vintage/Blush 662611.

Pages 78–81: designer: Rhea Crenshaw, Memphis, Tenn.; stylist: Julie Azar; photographer: Emily Minton; workroom: Unique Decor, Memphis, Tenn.; bed valance, bed drapery, chair: Norfolk Rose/Rose 662510; bed drapery lining, windows, table topper rosettes: Ivy League/Crimson 662701; window valances, drapery piping, bed skirt, table topper: Fairhaven/Rose 662623; bedspread: Roman Holiday/Natural 631080; wallpaper: Addie/Berry 570433.

Page 82: photos 1, 4, 6: stylist: Heather Lobdell; photographer: Jeff McNamara; accessories: Waverly Home; rug, lamps by Waverly. photo 3, photographer: Emily Minton.

Page 84: Waverly patterns for Butterick; left: wallpaper: Appleton Stripe/Pearl 569180; shade: Cambria/Rosewood 663362, trim: Silken Stripe/Rosewood 663382; right: color Indigo; wallpaper: Hillsdale Stripe 571202; valance: Wall Street 662712; shade: Hillsdale Vintage 662602.

Page 85: Waverly patterns for Butterick; left: wallpaper: Pick Me/Cobalt 570480; valance: Oak Bluff/French Blue 602684; shade: Vineyard Check/French Blue 602544; right: color Chambray; wallpaper: General Store 571031; shade: Old Mill Inn Vintage 662172, Bedford Stripe Vintage 662172.

Page 88: color Charcoal except as noted; wallpaper: Farmstead 572065, Renfrew Stripe 571385, Farmstead Border 572075; chair: Farmstead 663255; bed skirt: McCheck/Black 608025; window shade, comforter reverse: Classic Ticking/Black 605225; comforter: Country Life/Black 659433.

Pages 90–93: photos courtesy of Better Homes and Gardens® Special Interest Publications® *Quick and Easy Decorating*™ Spring/Summer 1999.

Pages 94–97: designer: Michael Buchanan; stylist: Cynthia Doggett; photographer: Tria Giovan; window panel, pillow: Lynnbrook/Claret 663721; valance: Country Fair/Crimson 662682; sofa: Spinakker Stripe/Rose 630817; pillows: Pantry Plaid/Crimson 662672, Jester/Claret 600001, Fernwood Vintage/Crimson 662642; accessories: Waverly Home.

Page 98: drapery: Dalton Stripe/Lagoon 662284; sofa: Compton/Flame 662292; table skirt: Brookville/Spring 601474; upholstered chair: Dunham 662245; wallpaper: Clifford/Cream 564717.

Pages 100–101: left: see page 23; right: all fabrics, color Bordeaux; drapery: Lorenzo 664440; chairs, pillows: Medici 664480; ottoman: Prato 664510; sofa: Ferrari Stripe 664530; pillows: Galileo 664500, Florin 664490; wallpaper: Palma/Suede 564072.

Page 102: wallpaper: color Pine; Davanzetti 571631, Delancey Stripe 569428; border: Davanzetti Border 571621; chairs: Emily/Topaz 602206; window: Rivoli/Champagne 614821

Page 105: designer: Rhea Crenshaw; stylist: Julie Azar; photographer: Emily Minton; tablecloth: Bremen/Shrimp 663913; draperies: Ottoman/Khaki 647007.

Pages 106–107: designer: Sally H. Draughon, Previews Interior Designs, Macon, Ga.; photographer: Emily Minton; draperies: Brilliant/Lemon 602123; table runner: Greenbriar Damask/Persimmon 631546; chair seats: Chaplin/Straw 601105, Chaplin/Tomato 601102.

Pages 108–11: designer, stylist: Elizabeth Dooner; photographer: Emily Minton; wallpaper: Country Life Lattice/Black 569883; drapery: Easy Elegance Diamonds/Ivory 609514; sheers: Miller/Champagne 614831; bed skirt, Eurshams: Picnic Check/Black 630266; pillow trim: Designer Gimp/Black 304417; bolsters, pillow: Devon Check/Black 630377; white pillows: Admiral/Natural 601000; toile pillows: Garden Toile/Onyx 664572; red pillows: Dominica/Poppy 600983; coverlet, chair: Arcadia/Black 601551; zebra rug by Martha Virden, Leland, Miss.

Pages 112–13: designer, stylist: Elizabeth Dooner; photographer: Emily Minton; walls: Waverly paint WA156/Olive; coverlet: Chandler from The Luxury Collection; Eurshams, duvet, drapery, neck roll pillow: Windsor Washed Velvet/Toffee 631561; pillows, bed skirt: Mountaineer/Brick 631614; green pillows: Windsor Washed Velvet/Taffy, Copper Olive 631572; leopard pillow: Rondeau/Natural 660090; chair and ottoman: Bouclette/Wheat 603130.

Pages 114–15: designer: Michael Buchanan; stylist: Cynthia Doggett; photographer: Tria Giovan; chair, headboard: Greenbriar Damask/Fawn 631542; Regal Rose bedding ensemble from The Luxury Collection by Waverly: comforter, shams: Palace Scroll/Taupe, bed skirt Regal Rose/Chocolate, solid shams: Havilande; chair pillows: Regal Rose/Chocolate 664250, Greenbriar Damask/Fawn 631542; Castle/Oatmeal 601062; needlepoint pillow: Yew Too/Sage by Waverly Home Fashions; pillow on bed: Capulet/Ecru 647321; bed pillow flap, valance: Regal Rose/Chocolate 664250; roman shades: Palace Scroll/Taupe 664260; sheer bed curtains, windows: Balcony/Cream 631330; accessories: Waverly Home.

Pages 116–17: left: curtains: Parma/Copper 664523; chair: Lorenzo/Pewter 664443; canopy: Turino Stripe/Copper 664453; comforter, pillows: Firenze/Pewter 647503; pillows: Florin/Pewter 664493, Galileo/Pewter 664503; wallpaper: Vertical Strié/Natural 557390; center: curtains, pillows, ottoman, comforter reverse: Regal Rose/Pine 664253; chair, pillows: Regiment Stripe/Topaz 664325; pillow shams, comforter: Palace Scroll/Pine 664263; pillows: Royal Crest/Pine 664273; blanket: Foularde/Topaz 664315; bed skirt: Royal Crest/Pine 664273; right: Prague bedding ensemble by Waverly Home Fashion; comforter, Euroshams, pillows, draperies: Prague/Document; dust ruffle: Dresden/ Parchment; flanged shams: Prague/Parchment; pillows: Dresden/Parchment; bed linens, pillows: by Waverly.

Pages 118–21: designer: Darlene M. Siwik, ASID allied member, Interiors by Design, Barrington, Ill.; stylist, Elaine Markoutsas; photographer: James Yochum; walls: Fleurette/Plum 609337; bed curtain, table cover: Pageantry/Sage 663871; bed curtain lining and canopy: Tate Check/Chestnut 602344; armchair slipcovers: Cheetah/Copper 600011; queen shams: Saxony/Forest 609565; duvet: Doylestown/Buttercream 603033; throw: Florentine/Boxwood 602233; Euroshams, bed skirt, drapery border: Empress/Moss 631819; draperies: Baltic Brocade/Berry 664053; shades: Ivy League/Mulberry 662705; chair seat, neck roll: Alexandra/Bottle 602247; paisley pillow: Pemberton/Indigo 602312; canopy welt and ties: Retro Denim/Claret 370539; chair pillows: Elsa/Linen 603090; Designer Gimp/Taupe 304411; Designer Loop Fringe/Taupe 304421; bed sheets: Anichini Inc.; armoire: Vintage Pine, Ltd., Chicago; rug: Oriental Rugs International, Chicago; accessories: The March Collection, Geneva, Ill., Embelezar and Pavilion, Chicago; bed/drapery workroom: Barbara Glass, Fancy Drapery Workroom, Lake Zurich, Ill.; upholstered walls: Anne Marie Ltd.

Pages 122–23: Photos 1, 4: stylist, Elaine Markoutsas; photographer James Yochum; photo 2: stylist, Elizabeth Dooner; photographer, Emily Minton; cushions: Ferrari Stripe/Venetian Green 664532; photos 3, 8: stylist, Julie Azar; photographer, Emily Minton; photo 5: photographer: Cheryle Dalton; photos 6, 9: Waverly Home; lamp, rug by Waverly; stylist, Heather Lobdell; photographer: Jeff McNamara.

Page 124: left: wallpaper: Wilmont/Taupe 573442, Linwood Stripe/Taupe 573435; border: Signature Border/Charcoal 572652; right: see page 21.

Page 125: left: color Plum, except as noted; wallpaper: Prague 573081, Prague Stripe 573111, Prague Mini 573101; border: Prague Border 573091; pillows: Prague 663881, Luxurious/Birch 630423; right: see page 18.

Page 128: curtains: Simple Stripe/Cobalt 664422; table skirts: Cherry Blossom/Cobalt 664381; table topper and slipcovers: Check It Out/Cherry 664404; books: Check It Out/Forest 664405; wallpaper: Cherry Blossom/Cobalt 573931, Cherry Plaid/Cobalt 573951; border: Cherry Plaid Border/Cobalt 573941.

Pages 130–35: designer, stylist: Catherine Kramer, Des Moines, Ia.; photographer: Hopkins Associates; walls: Waverly paints: WT110 Buttercream, WP237 Azure Blue, WD238 Delft; sofa: Party Plaid/Sky 647304; chairs: Ottoman/Royal 647020; pillows: Old World Linen/Daffodil 645606, Aqua 645625, Delft 645621, Federal 645620, Navy 645622; sheers: Marvelous/Ivory 370002, Cadet 370018; table runner: Chubby Check/Rainbow 663613; ottoman: Hideaway/Chambray 661632; overdoor valance: Parfait/Sky 663981; chair pads, napkins by Waverly.

Page 136: stylist, Heather Lobdell; photographer: Jeff McNamara; accessories: Waverly Home; lampshade: Pastoral Plaid/Grass; sofa, pillows: Playful Plaid/Grass 603003; chair, ottoman, pillow: Charming Check/Grass 602993; chair pillows: Playful Plaid/Sunshine 603004, Cheery

Cherries/Rainbow; draperies: Fruit Salad/Lemonlime 663930.

Page 138: See page 15.

Pages 140–43: designer, stylist: Catherine Kramer; photographer: Hopkins Associates; walls: Waverly paints WP136 Snow White, colorwashed with WD303 Lichen; table: WT102 Saffron Yellow, WA202 Cherry, WD222 Smokey Violet; sofa and lamp shade motifs: 664370; shades: Limerick/White 647091; swags and banding on shades: 664423; chair seats: Limerick/Ruby 647106; chair seat skirts and fabric picture mats: Check It Out/Cherry 664404; register cushion and fabric picture mats: Check It Out 664401; area rug: Limerick/Nile 647119, Limerick/Khaki 647096; solid pillows: Old World Linen/Daffodil 645606, Navy 645622.

Page 144: color Grass except as noted; table runner: Playful Plaid 603003, Glorious Garden; 663524; chairs: Pastoral Plaid 663534, Second Spring/Sunshine 663502, Playful Plaid 603003; sheers: Miller/White 614830; trim: Glorious Garden 663524.

Page 146: Waverly pattern for Butterick; wallpaper: Garden Leaf/Leaf 572192; chairs: Midsummer/Watermelon 663901; table skirt: Vacation/Watermelon 663811; table topper: Picnic/Watermelon 663791; trim: Perfection/Spice 647201.

Pages 148–49: wallpaper: Demitasse Companion/Lake 572211, Demi Check/Porcelain 572220, Demitasse Border/Lake 572201; chairs: Demitasse/Lake 663541; tablecloth: Perfection/French Blue 647207; table topper: Perfection/Buttercream 647198; trim, piping on chairs: Wickerwork/Royal 660872.

Pages 150–51: left: wallpaper: color Aqua; Blossomtime 573350; borders: Blossomtime Border 573360, Doina 573413; windows, chair skirts: Blossomtime/Aqua 663780; valance, chair pads: Heritage/Chambray 647070; chair skirt trim and ties: Heritage/Barn Red 647066; center: wallpaper: Berry Toss/Bright 574251, Bountiful Check/Lemonlime 572178; border: Parfait Border/Lemonlime 574220; window: Party Plaid/Marigold 647301; place mats: Fruit Salad/Lemonlime 663930; napkins, slipcovers: Parfait/Lemonlime 663980; right: wallpaper: Botanica/Victorian 571470; border: Botanica Border/Victorian 571510; chairs, pillows, table runner: Parlour Plaid/Poppy 600723.

Page 152: color Document; wallpaper: Check It Out 573870, Kitsch Kitchen 573830; border: Kitsch Kitchen Border 573840 ; bench pad, curtain, napkin: Simple Stripe 664420; tablecloth: Check It Out 664400; right: see page 128.

Page 154: comforter, pillow shams: Spring Fling/Aqua 663800; chair, ottoman: Vacation/Aqua 663810; pillows: Midsummer/Lime 663900; drapery: Blossomtime/Aqua 663780; upholstered .sleigh bed: Picnic/Lime 663794

Page 156: color Natural; comforter, shams, pillows: Second Spring 663500; comforter (reverse), draperies: Pastoral Plaid 663530; bed skirt, shams: Glorious Garden 663520; background pillow: Summer Studies 663510.

Page 157: wallpaper: color Grass; Trellis Toss 572453; borders: Glorious Garden Border 572493, Pastoral Plaid Border 572473; chair: Glorious Garden/Sunshine 663522; pillows, sham: Pastoral Plaid/Grass 663534; comforter, shams, bed linens: Summer Studies by Waverly.

Pages 158–59: designer, stylist: Catherine Kramer; photographer: Hopkins Associates; duvet: Checkmate/Sunwashed 664215; dust ruffle and folding screen panel: Glosheen/Bluebell 645531; screen panels: Glosheen; pillows: Garden Trellis/Vanilla 664171.

Pages 160–61: comforter: Just Leaves/Leaf 664161; shams: Just Leaves/Leaf 664161; flange: Block Party/Celedon 664200; bed skirt: Block Party/Celedon 664200; throw pillows: Party Plaid/Natural 647300; throw: Ranger/Basil 609843; border and ottoman: Arbor Day/Leaf 664151; chair pillow: Checkmate/Celedon 664210; windows: Starlight/White 631310; border: Checkmate/Celedon 664210.

Page 162: color Sky; table skirt: Parfait 663981, border: Block Party 664204; seat cushion: Checkmate 664214.

Pages 164-65: designer: Michael Buchanan; stylist: Cynthia Doggett; photographer: Tria Giovan; seat cushions: Floral Festival/Garden 663971; table toppers: Check It Out/Cobalt 664403; table skirts: Floral Festival/Garden 663971; pillows: Check It Out/Cobalt 664403, Floral Festival/Sky 663971, Picnic/Lemon 663792; umbrella: Picnic/Lemon 663792.

Pages 166-67: designer: Deborah Hastings; photographer: Emily Minton; seat cushions: Spring Fling/Lemon 663802; napkins Vacation/Lemon 663812, by Waverly.

Pages 168-71: designer: Deborah Hastings; photographers: Emily Minton, Howard Lee Puckett; dust ruffle, valance: Picnic/Aqua 663790; shams: Spring Fling/Aqua 663800, piping Harmony/Peony 655934, ruffle and dressing table chair: Vacation/Aqua 663810; bed curtains, café curtains: Blossomtime/ Aqua 663780; table skirt: Spring Fling/Aqua 663800 with Miller/White 614830 overlay; wicker chair seat cushion: Glosheen/Nugget 645509, piping Harmony/Peony 655934.

Page 172: Photos 1, 3, 4, 5, 8, 9: stylist, Catherine Kramer; photographer, Hopkins Associates.

Pages 174: left: Castille bedding ensemble from The Luxury Collection by Waverly; comforter, shams, breakfast pillow: Castille/Jewel; bed skirt, Eurosham: Heritage/Topaz; drapery panel, coverlet: Chandler; throw pillow: Aragon/Jewel; right: Pageantry bedding ensemble from The Luxury Collection by Waverly; duvet, shams, neck roll, throw pillow: Pageantry/Buttercream; bed skirt, Eurosham: Greenwich Plaid/Lemongrass; solid coverlet, shams: Havilande.

Pages 175: left: Meadow Way bedding ensemble from The Luxury Collection by Waverly; duvet: Meadow Way/Buttercream; bed skirt, Eurosham: Nichole Plaid/Apple; shams, pillows: Nichole/ Apple, Nichole Check, Nichole Solid; solid coverlet, shams: Emma; right: Just Leaves bedding ensemble from The Luxury Collection by Waverly; duvet, Euroshams, breakfast pillow: Arbor Day/Leaf; bed skirt, shams: Homespun/Natural; throw pillow: Just Leaves/Leaf.

Pages 182-87: designer: Rhea Crenshaw; stylist: Julie Azar; photographer: Emily Minton; sofa: Dominica/Chili 600981; draperies, accent pillows, upholstered chairs: Garden Lane/Salmon 663393; sheers: Peter Pan 370140; table skirts: Gazebo Check/Poppy 600733; table toppers, chair seats: Pretty Petals/Salmon 663403; chair seat, pillow: Midland Check/Paprika 600970; buffet skirt: Canterbury/Antique 661714; window shades: Paradise Plaid/Sunburst 600712; dining chair skirts: Lunette/Stem 600965.

Page 188: sofa, cushions: Lynnbrook/Topaz 663723; window treatments: Westbourne/Claret 663672; pillows on sofa: Easton Gate/Claret 663692; chair and pillow on sofa: Highgrove/Topaz 647243; pillow on chair: Prescott/Topaz 663685.

Pages 190–91: designer: Rhea Crenshaw; stylist: Julie Azar; photographer: Emily Minton; sofa: Ranger/Maize 630002; draperies, side-chair seats, pillow trim, skirted table: Hanover/Colonial 661080; skirted table pleats, armchair: Tate Check/Bottle 602345; skirted armchair: Arcadia.

Pages 192–93: designer: Sally Draughon.; photographer: Emily Minton; window shades and table skirt: Glorious Garden 663524; valances and table top: Summer Studies 663514; upholstered chair and ottoman: Northport/Punch 601491; armchairs: Greenbriar Damask/Persimmon 631546.

Page 194: wallpapers: Marbury Stripe/Leaf 573221, Marbury Vine/Leaf 574123; border: Marbury Border/Leaf 573213; sofa: Juliette/Spearmint 647186; ottoman, pillow: Marbury /Leaf 663563; chair: Wesley/Leaf 663563.

Page 195: pillow, window treatment, chair (foreground): Artistry/Linen 663831; screen: Opal/Linen 663841; cushions, table topper: Juliette/Tangerine 647181; upholstered chair: Romeo/Tangerine 647231.

Page 196: wallpaper: Country Life/Garnet 564300; window treatments: Selections by Waverly Home Fashions: Monroe valance, Hancock panel in Tattersall/Colonial; table skirt, chair pad: Country Life/Garnet 659430.

Pages 198-99: designer, stylist: Deborah Hastings; photographer: Emily Minton; slipcovers: Miller/White 614830; table and buffet runners: Romeo Plaid/Lilac 647320.

Page 200: wallpaper: Abigail/Indigo 570912, General Store/Chambray 571031; border: Brenden Border/Indigo 562009; pillows: Abigail/Indigo 662692, Country Fair/Indigo 662684, Old Mill Inn Vintage/Chambray 662172; windows, table topper: Old Mill Inn Vintage/Chambray 662172; table skirt: Antique Fair/Chambray 662760.

Page 201: (left) color Buttercream except as noted; wallpaper: Gazebo Companion 574043; border: Mini Gazebo Border 574053; drapery: Simple Stripe/Apple 664421; chairs, table: Gazebo 664413.

Pages 202-203: designer, stylist: Carla Breer Howard; photographer: Jon Jensen; banquette: Picket Fence/Cream 601710; workroom: Michael's Custom Built, Inc., San Rafael, Calif.; paisley pillows: Hillsdale Vintage/Crimson 662601; blue pillows: Tapestry/Mist 646087, trim Designer Natural 6 Bullion/Natural 304230; floral inset pillows: Perfection/Mist 647209, Hanover/Coral 661084; workroom: Georgina Rice & Co., San Francisco; slipcovers: Perfection/Mist 647209; cord trim: Perfection/Natural 647192; appliqué motif: Hanover/Coral 661084; workroom: Laurel Sprigg Custom Interior Sewing, San Francisco.

Pages 204-207: designer: Sally Draughon; photographer: Emily Minton; draperies, bedspread, pillow shams, table skirt: 661455; bed skirt, pillows, bench: 600723.

Pages 208-209: designer: Rhea Crenshaw; stylist: Julie Azar; photographer: Emily Minton; color Chambray except as noted; wallpaper: Carmela 571153; love seat and draperies: Romance 663453; table toppers, duvet: Enchantress 663443; table skirts: Candlewicking/Natural 645980; dust ruffle: Spring Song 663463.

Pages 210-11: left: color Loden except as noted; drapery, comforter, pillow shams: Roseberry 663770; chair: Pembridge 663760; bed skirt, ruffled shams: Penrose 663700; table skirt: Prescott 663680; pillow: Highgrove 647247; bed curtains: Castlebury/Pistachio 663713; center: comforter, window treatments: Lucinda/Citron 662450; pillows: General Store/Fern 662782, Country Club/Fern 662821, Country Club/Crimson 662822, Cozy/Fern 601433, Cranston Plaid/Spruce 602223; right: wallpaper: Lucinda/Citron 570840, Everett Stripe/Citron 571390; border: Lucinda Border/Citron 570850; comforter, chair, pillow: Lucinda/Citron 662450; ottoman: Country Club/Fern 662821; pillows: Country Fair/Crimson 662682, General Store/Fern 662782, Country Fair/Fern 662682.

Page 212: designer: Rhea Crenshaw; stylist: Julie Azar; photographer: Emily Minton; wallpaper: Camilla/Sage 572892; window shade: Castlebury/Stone 663711.

Page 213: wallpaper: Rose Scent Stripe/Victorian 572350, Petite Rose/Victorian 572360; border: Rose Scent Border/Victorian 572330; chairs, window: Farmstead/Grass 663257.

Page 214: chaise, drapery trim: Country Club/Fern 662821; drapery: Peter Pan/Natural 370140; table skirt, pillows: Lucinda/Citron 662450; pillow left: Country Fair/Fern 662685; chair pad: Country Fair/Crimson 662682.

Pages 216-17: designer: Rhea Crenshaw; stylist: Julie Azar; photographer: Emily Minton; folding screen, seat cushions: Westbourne/Loden 663670; scalloped table topper, pillows: Highgrove/Loden 647247; table skirt, round pillow: Prescott/Apple 663682; plaid envelope pillow, iron chair cushion: Cabin Plaid/Laurel 602422.

Pages 218-21: designer, stylist: Carla Breer Howard; photographer: Jon Jensen; table skirt, umbrella liner: Dalton Stripe/Primrose 662280; umbrella liner workroom: Georgina Rice & Co.; table topper: Newstead-Chintz/Parrot 660150; reversible chair cushions: Newstead Sun 'N Shade/Parrot 664140, Manor Plaid Sun 'N Shade/Ivy 664100; hammock pad: Newstead Sun 'N Shade/Parrot; workroom: Stoich Designs, Larkspur, Calif.; napkins, toss pillows: Party Plaid/Poppy 647302.

Page 222: Photos 1, 2, 3, 5, 7, 8, 9: photographer: Emily Minton; accessories private collections; photos 4, 6: stylist, Heather Lobdell; photographer: Jeff McNamara; accessories: Waverly Home; photo 4, rug by Waverly.